Contents

Acknowledgements

We wish to thank John Mansfield, Senior Inspector for Special Educational Needs in the London Borough of Sutton, for suggesting to us that a study on educational provision for disaffected teenagers would be a worthwhile one. We are also greatly indebted to the many members of staff belonging to local authority support services, colleges and off-site units who gave so generously of their time in completing questionnaires, receiving us on visits, and talking to us about their work with disaffected pupils in Key Stage 4.

In order to preserve confidentiality, we promised to mention no names, but a list of participating authorities and institutions is given in the Appendices.

Introduction

In the summer of 1991, a London borough decided to close the off-site unit for Year 11 pupils who had been excluded from schools, no longer attended regularly, or were clearly not benefiting from mainstream provision. In common with a number of similar institutions set up by most authorities from the mid-1970s onwards, the unit was now seen to marginalize its clientele and to be too small to deliver a broad-based curriculum sufficient to meet the demands of Key Stage 4. The unit, of which one of us had been in charge for 12 years, is now being replaced by a Year 11 project in which staff call upon a range of resources such as work experience and courses in further education. The same team also provides 'outreach' support for teachers in the classroom as well as intervention strategies for younger secondary pupils who are showing signs of persistent misbehaviour.

This personal situation prompted a previous publication, *Teaching Troubled and Troublesome Adolescents* (Lovey, 1992), which was informed not only by the experiences of running an off-site unit but also by a small-scale study of some units in other authorities (Lovey, 1991). These factors were also instrumental in bringing about the present national survey of local authority provision for the education of disaffected 14–16-year-olds.

In Chapter 1, we outline the background to the present predicaments faced by schools and local authorities with respect to adolescents presenting behaviour problems in Years 10 and 11. We discuss the current controversies surrounding the debate about the reportedly rising numbers of exclusions from schools, and trace the developments which have put authorities under pressure to develop alternative strategies to the off-site support unit, so favoured in the late 1970s and early 1980s but whose educational and economic viability is now seriously questioned.

In Chapter 2, we describe the aims and methods of our investigation, which involved sending a questionnaire to all local authorities in England, a supplementary questionnaire to selected authorities to elicit perceptions of particular practices, plus a series of personal interviews and visits to various institutions. Our findings are reported in Chapters 3 to 6. In the final chapter, we highlight the main issues brought out by the study in terms of current practice and recent initiatives, and suggest possible ways forward.

Although the value of this investigation is limited by the failure of many local authorities to reply to our enquiries, we hope that the contributions generously made by numerous individuals in the responding authorities will facilitate the dissemination of ideas and help to contribute to the development of strategies which effectively address the problem of disaffection among pupils in their last year of secondary school.

CHAPTER 1

Current Predicaments and Changing Practices

This study was conceived against the background of two prevailing sets of policies within the education service. Although both were promoted by Conservative administrations with the common objective of raising educational standards and opportunities, they are frequently perceived by the teaching profession as existing in a state of mutual tension, creating dilemmas for schools in their dealings with pupils presenting behaviour problems.

On the one hand are the policies associated with the integrationist movement, whose supporters argue that all pupils should have right of access to mainstream provision unless they are among the highly exceptional few whose needs are such that they can realistically only be met in special schools or units. On this argument, ordinary schools should be given the necessary resources to develop more effective pro-active strategies and provision for personal support, so helping to reduce the number of pupils who are excluded or institutionally segregated in special behavioural units.

Alongside this integrationist approach is the Government's crusade to raise standards by promoting competition between schools. Among other things, this involves publishing tables of schools' achievements, insisting that school budgets are based essentially on levels of enrolment, and encouraging the creation of a separate tier of self-governing schools to compete with those remaining under local authority control.

Head teachers and governing bodies have been quick to recognize the stark reality of this open marketplace approach with its life-threatening chain reaction. In this, behaviour problems and truancy adversely affect the attainment of both the perpetrators and those learning alongside them. This in turn makes the school vulnerable to its position in

1

published league tables of achievement, attendance and first destinations, with the associated risk of adverse publicity lowering the school's public image and, as a consequence, prospects of healthy enrolment. Any reduction in pupil numbers in turn reduces the school's budget through the pupil-led funding formula and presages staff redundancies. Faced by this domino effect, some schools ask why, in the interests of survival, they should dither in refusing and excluding budget-bashing pupils today if such reticence is to discourage the recruitment of budget-boosting pupils tomorrow. It seems that the Government's flagship policies of choice and diversity have persuaded many secondary schools to be less tolerant both in containing unconforming pupils and in accepting those with a record of behaviour problems in other schools.

The problem has given rise to a number of controversial cases, as illustrated by two in Conservative-controlled Barnet. In one of these, the governors of Mill Hill County High School sent a letter to parents urging them to vote for grant-maintained status partly on the grounds that the school could then 'refuse entry to known troublemakers' (*TES*, 3 July 1992). In a parallel case, the Education Secretary was asked to investigate complaints by 12 parents of former pupils at Queen Elizabeth Boys Grant-maintained School that there had been 'a calculated campaign to get rid of their sons' (*TES*, 31 July 1992).

The predicaments generated by the tension between the two Government policies outlined above have been accentuated by a stream of negative reports about schools in the media. In shaping public opinion on the state of the education service, the role of the popular press – notably the *Daily Mail* and its counterpart on Sunday – cannot be ignored. As well as being debated among the commuters and coffee morning population of the leafy shires, these tabloid reports have been chewed over on the popular Jimmy Young show on Radio 2 and highlighted in evening news bulletins on TV. The effect of much of this has been to agitate public anxieties about educational standards and to depress the morale and status of teachers yet further. Unfortunately, examples of demonstrably good practice do not have the same newsworthiness.

Concern about the numbers of pupils being excluded from school was expressed in the Government's White Paper *Choice and Diversity* (DfE, 1992a), and the Discussion Paper on Exclusions published towards the end of the same year recognized the unsatisfactoriness of the situation in no uncertain terms:

Too many children are excluded from school, either permanently or temporarily.

There is evidence that some exclusions go on too long, and that the alternative educational provision made for many excluded pupils is subject to unacceptable variations in both quality and quantity (DfE, 1992b, para.1)

We now turn to examine each of the issues that are acknowledged in this statement:

- the scale of the problem;

- abuses of the system; and

- the suitability of provision.

Dismissing Disaffection: The Problem of Escalating Exclusions

A number of recent surveys have suggested a marked, and possibly increasing, reluctance among many secondary heads to embrace policies of containment and intervention and instead to engage in damage-limitation by excluding pupils more freely. Since regular truants can ruin a school's attendance record, some pupils are even excluded for not coming to school!

In the summer of 1990, through the National Exclusions Reporting System (NERS), the DfE began a two-year study to monitor permanent exclusions from LEA and grant-maintained schools. This was the first official effort to collect information systematically on a nationwide scale. Unfortunately, as senior department officials have admitted, the data may not be reliable since the NERS relies on self-reports from schools (*TES*, 25 September 1992). Additionally, the survey does not include temporary exclusions or schools in the independent sector.

The analysis of the findings (DfE News 126/93) revealed that permanent exclusions rose from 2,910 in 1990/91 to 3,833 in 1991/92, a rise of 32 per cent. Boys outnumbered girls by 4:1 in year one and 5:1 in year two. Those in the primary sector increased from 13 to 14 per cent of the total, while those with special needs increased from 12.5 to 15 per cent.

However, the exclusion rates differed markedly between schools. Although this could be attributed in part to socio-economic differences in catchment areas, the variations were said to be too large to be explained by this factor alone. This view is consistent with the conclusions drawn in regional studies on exclusions by Galloway *et al* . (1985) in Sheffield, McManus (1987) in Leeds, and Imich in Essex (*TES*, 23 October 1992). Indeed, McManus found that it was often schools with the highest proportions of deprived, working-class children that had the lowest exclusion rates; while Imich (in an address to the annual conference of the Association of Educational Psychologists in the autumn of 1992) reported that two schools in his county accounted for as much as 50 per cent of all permanent exclusions, while another school accounted for 35 per cent.

In the DfE analysis, the main reasons for exclusion turned out to be refusal to comply with school rules and verbal abuse or insolence to teachers. Next in importance was physical aggression and bullying (which emerged as the main reason in the Essex study mentioned above), though physical aggression against school staff was 'relatively rare'.

Among other evidence about the scale of the exclusions problem are two recent teacher union surveys which attracted considerable media attention. The more alarmist, published by the National Union of Teachers (1992) but based on research by consultants Coopers and Lybrand Deloitte, suggested that during 1990/91, exclusions of all types had risen by as much as one-fifth, with an estimated 25,000 pupils suspended or expelled. The increase (which the NUT maintained was an underestimate of the real position since not all authorities included temporary suspensions in their returns) was attributed mainly to pressure on resources and the impending introduction of published league tables comparing school performances. These factors, together with 'deteriorating home circumstances and lack of parental discipline' (p.5), were said to be restricting the ability of schools – as well as their motivation – to make suitable on-site provision for their disaffected pupils. However, the NUT estimate must be treated with some caution since it was based on returns from just 26 of the 117 local authorities in England and Wales.

At about the same time, another study was published by the Secondary Heads Association (1992). This covered almost 800 secondary institutions, and included grant-maintained and independent schools as well as those run by local councils. In contrast to the NUT, the SHA was non-committal about the possibility that suspension and expulsion rates were rising, pointing out that the level of permanent exclusions was low – 1.8 pupils per thousand – though the rate for all categories was 22 per thousand. However, like the DfE and Essex studies referred to above, the SHA emphasized that the incidence varied widely, around two-thirds of permanent exclusions coming from a quarter of schools.

The SHA found no evidence that large schools tend to exclude more than small ones. However, compared with local authority schools, those that were independent or grant-maintained were found to have admitted fewer pupils who had been excluded from other schools or who were 'at risk' of being so. The figures were taken to lend some substance to fears that 'LEA schools will become "dumping grounds" for the most difficult pupils' (SHA, 1992, p.5), with LEA heads running 'sink' schools in a two-tier system as more schools opt out of council control.

In contrast to the SHA caution over claims of escalating exclusions, other reports have talked about rates doubling or more. Among these have been the Association of Metropolitan Authorities (*TES*, 26 June 1992), the Association of Educational Psychologists (*TES*, 23 October 1992), the Advisory Centre for Education (1992) and a MORI poll for BBC's *Panorama* (15 March 1993). ACE reported that the proportion of phone calls from parents about exclusions had risen during the last four months of 1991 from 8 to 17 per cent The later MORI poll, based on a return from 79 of the 127 local education authorities in England, Wales and Scotland, estimated that temporary suspensions and permanent expulsions were now running at the rate of 66,000 per year. This represented an increase of 50 per cent during the two-year period between 1990/91 and 1991/2, compared with the earlier NUT (1992) estimate of a 20 per cent increase during 1990/91. Forty-two per cent of LEAs in the MORI poll cited the new climate of competition between schools as the main reason for the escalation in exclusion rates, while 22 per cent attributed the increased figures to demands arising from the National Curriculum and other recent legislation, which left less time to deal with behaviour problems. Significantly, only 8 per cent maintained that poorer discipline *per se* was the key factor. According to the Office for Standards in Education, the rise in exclusions is steady in most authorities, with a notable increase in numbers of pupils excluded from primary schools (Ofsted, 1993).

Acknowledging the scale of the problem, the Government and its advisers have been suggesting ways in which schools could be persuaded to keep pupils who might otherwise be excluded. In a consultation document on performance-related pay published in June 1992, the School Teachers' Review Body (STRB) suggested that teachers in schools with low exclusion rates might be given extra remuneration for their efforts in containing the situation and that, conversely, schools with high rates should be penalized through the pay structures. In the event, these suggestions were received dismissively by the Government because the STRB approach to discretionary pay supplements was based on the achievements of school staff as a body rather than on those of individual teachers. However, the DfE Discussion Paper published the same year (DfE, 1992b) suggested other possible means whereby schools might be encouraged to exclude more sparingly.

One idea was to require schools to publish their exclusion figures along with other measures of performance in the annual league tables. Presumably it was thought that such a requirement would make heads more circumspect before excluding a pupil – though some prospective pupils' parents might be more impressed by the high excluding school which they perceive as taking much-needed tough action. The DfE recognized, however, that publication of exclusion rates could have two disadvantageous effects. It might serve to discourage teachers from recommending exclusion in cases where such action would be 'an appropriate response to a particular individual disciplinary problem' (para. 31); and it could tempt schools to pressurize parents into withdrawing their children 'voluntarily' and so save having to record an exclusion formally. Other DfE suggestions involved adjustments to schools' budgets, possibly mid-year. For instance, schools could be offered financial support for 'difficult and disruptive pupils'. As the DfE recognized, this could lead to problems of definition for the purposes of formula funding, but it would at least go some way in providing schools with the extra resources needed to make more appropriate provision for pupils with behaviour problems. More contentiously, and to the outrage of the teacher unions, the DfE mooted the possibility that schools might be 'fined', not only losing the funding for the excluded pupil but also multiples of that amount.

Given that the size of a school's budget is now based mainly on pupil numbers, it is only fair that money should immediately follow the excluded pupil to his new school. But it is difficult to see the justice in 'fining' schools for excluding pupils as a genuine last resort or for lack of resources to devote to problem behaviour. Apart from undermining the governing body's position in running a school, a head should not be penalized for excluding a pupil who, despite all efforts by the staff, is damaging the education or well-being of other pupils. Moreover, it has to be recognized that some children's extreme behaviour is a cry for help, and that exclusion can sometimes break a pattern of disaffection, prompt parents to take a more constructive role, and give the child a fresh start. There are also some pathologies, such as schizophrenia, manic depression and Huntingdon's Chorea, which develop in adolescence and cause difficult behaviour. The regular taking of amphetamines or so-called 'designer drugs' can also have this effect. No school should be fined for excluding a child whom the staff find unmanageable for such reasons.

Abuse of the Exclusions Facility and Failure to Follow Statutory Procedure

Legislation in the late 1980s did address one aspect of the exclusions problem by trying to inject some common justice into the procedures for suspending or expelling. The measures were a response to a series of well-publicized cases in which parents had not been properly informed about their child's exclusion or had found the appeal arrangements seriously wanting, or (as in the case of Poundswick High School, Manchester) intractable disputes had arisen over the LEA trying to reinstate a child against the school's wishes. Whilst the provisions relating to exclusion in the Education (No. 2) Act 1986 affect only LEA-maintained schools and not the independent sector, schools which have since become grant-maintained are subject to similar responsibilities by their articles of government (Model Article 13). As Stiles (1993) has observed,

> The law is designed to ensure that loss of education due to exclusion is minimized, that heads are not judges in their own cause and that parents know about the circumstances of exclusion, the type of exclusion [i.e. fixed term, indefinite or permanent], and what they need to do to ensure the resumption of education for their child.

The headteacher of a maintained school is statutorily obliged to inform the governors and local authority of any suspension which lasts for more than five school days in aggregate in any one term or which jeopardize the pupil's chance to take a public examination. Parents must be kept informed at all stages and given the right to make representations to governors and independent committees, while governing bodies and LEAs have powers to direct the reinstatement of pupils judged to have been unfairly excluded. Governors can also change the length of a fixed-term exclusion and decide how long an indefinite exclusion should last. In grant-maintained schools, it is the disciplinary committee of the governing body to which the head must supply information, to whom parents may appeal, and who may direct reinstatement.

According to the DfE, most schools seem to be following these procedures with care, at least in the case of permanent exclusions. In its analysis of returns to the National Exclusions Reporting System (DfE, 1992b), the Department reported that the vast majority of cases went unchallenged, governing bodies demanding reinstatement in less than 3 per cent of cases and LEAs in just over 4 per cent. Furthermore, in only 3 per cent of exclusions did the parents appeal, and then largely unsuccessfully.

It is possible, however, that governors and LEAs have a natural inclination to support their school's case and that many parents have not the stomach or the skills to mount a fight in the official appeals system. In any case, as the DfE also notes, there is other evidence from the NERS data which points to inconsistencies, prejudice and unfairness in some exclusion cases. In particular, Afro-Caribbean pupils are disproportionately represented, making up 8.1 per cent of all pupils permanently excluded, although they occupy only 2 per cent of the total school population. Comparable findings have been reported in other recent studies: ACE (1992), Cooper *et al.* (1991), Nottingham Education Department (1991) and Ofsted (1993). Also, as noted earlier, the DfE states that differences in exclusion rates between schools are greater than could be explained by socio-economic variations in catchment areas alone, suggesting that a pupil with a particular behaviour pattern would be more likely to be excluded from one school than another.

A further example of reported abuse of the system is the failure of some heads to inform the local education authority about exclusions which last more than a few days (Bennathan, 1992). Other cases involve incidents of unacceptable behaviour which were prompted by bullying and racial harassment; poor liaison between schools, LEAs and parents – including parents not being sent written notification of an exclusion and the reasons for it; differential treatment among children for comparable offences, some of which were about uniform and dress rather than serious incidents; and delays before governing bodies have heard appeals (ACE, 1992). In one recent case, a 12-year-old boy lost five months of schooling whilst his father spent £2,000 in legal fees fighting against his son's expulsion; an independent tribunal eventually demanded reinstatement since it found insufficient evidence for the governing body to have upheld the head's decision, which allegedly arose from an incident concerning cannabis (*TES*, 4 December 1992).

Both the Advisory Centre for Education and the Children's Legal Centre say that one of the main sources of complaint is parents who have been asked by the headteacher to find an alternative school for their child. Parents feel under pressure because a 'voluntary' change of school would mean no reference to exclusion on the child's record: the school is therefore saved having to justify a formal exclusion, but the parents lose their right to an appeal.

Provision for Excluded Pupils and Others with Behaviour Problems

Most secondary schools have some kind of support system for pupils presenting behaviour problems. Sometimes this is given only in crises, but more schools are now developing whole-school intervention policies in which staff work collaboratively to pre-empt the worst excesses of behaviour problems and share their expertise supportively with each other. Many schools also provide specially supervised facilities to allow a 'cooling off' period for pupils who are disruptive. Where intervention is developed in an integrated way, the strategies are not limited to skills in personal management, classroom control, and the reinforcement of wanted behaviour, but spill over into all aspects of school provision, not least curriculum planning.

Some pupils' behaviour is such that an application is made to the local authority for a multi-professional assessment of special educational need (SEN) under the 1981 Education Act. If a statement of SEN is given, extra resources may be provided within mainstream provision, or the pupil may be recommended for a place in a residential or day school for individuals with emotional and behavioural difficulties (EBD). Although such special school provision can be viewed as an infringement of integrationist principles, its supporters argue that we have to recognize the realities which behavioural problems present to mainstream staff. Some schools do manage to provide an ethos which does not add to the tensions which pupils bring from home, but others are less successful in this respect. Cooper (1992), for instance, insists that because 'some schools are simply unfit places for vulnerable children' (p. 23), special residential provision at best can offer 'a respite from problems located in the home situation', a 'high quality of staff-pupil relationships' and a 'process of re-signification, which is achieved through a wide range of opportunities for success and achievement' (p. 33).

But for pupils in their last year of secondary education (the focus of the present study), an application for statementing is rarely a practical proposition since there is insufficient time left for the statutory processing procedures. Also, as Bennathan (1992) has commented, some education authorities are now forbidding educational psychologists to recommend residential provision, not so much on ideological integrationist grounds but because of the high cost involved. Schools thus need recourse to some system which will lend immediate special support within the mainstream or give access to alternative provision outside it.

In an effort to keep as many pupils as possible in mainstream schools, 'Outreach' support has been developed in some local authorities. This provision is a much more recent initiative which, as Chapter 3 will show, is not yet developed on a large scale. In principle it can obviate the need for alternative provision, but mostly it is used to restrict the extent of its use.

Even with coordinated efforts to pre-empt school disciplinary crises through intervention strategies and sympathetic, individual attention, many teachers still find themselves with pupils in Year 11 who display general aggression and are offensive to staff and disrupt lessons. Some of these troubled and troublesome pupils end up being excluded from school, either temporarily or permanently, or stand in serious risk of being so. In law, the local authority has the duty to ensure that such pupils remain in ordinary schools or that they are given some kind of alternative provision. The parents maintain their right to choose a school, and the school is under its normal statutory obligation to meet the parents' wishes if it has room. However, this is frequently not a practicable proposition when the LEA has been removing spare places by closing or merging schools to use its resources more efficiently.

At the time of writing, the envisaged Education Act 1993 will give LEAs and other funding authorities the right to direct a school to admit a pupil who has not been found a place. Moreover, this power will apply to grant-maintained as well as LEA schools. The danger here is that LEAs may use their powers not for the good of the pupil or the school but because of the high cost of alternative provision. Also, schools receiving excluded pupils in Key Stage 4 may not be able to match the GCSE courses of the pupils' previous school.

Apart from being admitted to another mainstream school or to a special school, there are two main sorts of provision available for excluded pupils or others presenting behaviour problems which the school cannot manage effectively:

- individual tuition, full- or part-time (the term 'home' tuition is often a misnomer);

- placement outside school in an off-site unit, full- or part-time.

Individual tuition, as Bennathan (1992) has pointed out, was originally set up to maintain an education service for children who cannot attend school for a period because of health problems. It was not intended to offer support for behaviour problems, even though that is how it has sometimes come to be used. There is no DfE guidance about the amount of tuition time which pupils should be given: according to a recent inspectors' report, it can be as little as two hours a week, rarely exceeds ten, and is generally of poor quality (Ofsted, 1993). Also, the pupils remain the responsibility of the school, which also retains the funding for their educational provision.

Since the late 1970s, most education authorities have placed some excluded pupils or others with behaviour problems in off-site units. In the next section, we discuss the development of this provision and its problems.

Unfortunately, information about the kind of alternative provision made for excluded pupils has not always been given in the schools' returns to the national reporting system, and the DfE acknowledges that there are frequently lengthy delays both in making exclusions and in securing alternative provision. From the data available, however, the DfE claims that 29 per cent of pupils permanently excluded find a place in another mainstream school, while 44 per cent receive home tuition, 23 per cent are in special units, and 5 per cent are in special schools (DfE, 1992b). This accounts for 100 per cent – but other evidence suggests that many excluded children are no longer on anyone's books. In their survey report, the Secondary Heads Association (1992) estimated that one-quarter of those permanently excluded had not been readmitted to other schools. This statistic prompted the fear that, while some of these pupils would have been admitted to special units or given home tuition, others may have 'simply become detached from the school system' (p.3). This fear has more recently been confirmed in a report by Ofsted inspectors (1993) who cite one authority that had 'lost' 22 out of 86 excluded pupils.

The difficulties faced by local authorities in arranging suitable provision for disaffected pupils are compounded as delegation of budgets (now at least 85 per cent of the potential schools budget) and schools opting out reduce the funds available to provide support services. In terms of teacher-pupil ratios and time spent, provision for children with behavioural problems is expensive. LEA funds are also being stretched by more applications for statements of special need arising from behavioural problems. One writer (Pyke, 1992) has argued that,

> growing numbers of disruptive children are being defined as having 'emotional and behavioural difficulties', a catch-all category of special need that offers schools the chance to have pupils taken off their hands or to gain additional money. (p.14)

Segregating Disaffection: The Rise and Fall of the Off-site Unit

The burgeoning of special provision for disaffected pupils in the late 1970s and early 1980s was fuelled by the increased expectations of school discipline generated by the 'Great Debate' about educational standards. Inspired by Prime Minister Callaghan's Ruskin College speech in 1976, this was given further impetus by Sir Keith Joseph, the Education Secretary, in his address to the North of England Conference in 1984. By the beginning of the 1980s, an inquiry by the Advisory Centre for Education found a unit population of 5,857 pupils in 386 units among the 50 per cent of responding LEAs in the UK (ACE, 1980). In London the number of units doubled between 1978 and 1982 even though the school population in this period fell by 73,000 (ILEA, 1985).

However, as a series of surveys during this period revealed, the growth of off-site units was characterized by a piecemeal, totally individual and almost eccentric pattern of provision (Basini, 1981; HMI, 1978; Ling and Davies, 1984; Mortimer et al., 1983). There was some 'cross-fertilization' of good practice as some off-site staff used in-service opportunities to visit other units or moved to other authorities to gain promotion. However, it was not unusual for the staff of a unit to be unaware of comparable provision to theirs existing only a couple of miles away. On the whole, any sharing of information was done in a random way. An exception to this idiosyncratic growth was the termly meetings of teachers in the London Intermediate Treatment Association. Unfortunately, any of the IT units that survived all the difficulties of their situation were absorbed into local authority control and subsequently lost links with each other.

From the late 1980s, some authorities started moving away from segregated provision to greater in-school support (Drew, 1990). Even so, the Elton inquiry (DES, 1989) found that although a number of LEAs were planning to provide a more coherent support system by combining increased support in schools with reduced use of off-site units, only a few already had a continuum of provision in place. By the end of the 1980s, most authorities with units were planning to reorganize their off-site facilities on the basis of short-term placements for fewer pupils, while some had plans for complete closure (though Elton found that a few LEAs were expanding their alternative provision).

The demise of the off-site unit can be explained in part as a response to the acknowledged failings and limitations of segregated provision as revealed in various regional surveys and studies of individual units and centres during the 1980s (review in Docking, 1987). Much evidence, it is true, did demonstrate successful activity in off-site institutions. For instance, in their large-scale study of London units, Mortimore et al. (1983) found that only 4 per cent of the 162 pupils interviewed complained about their new situation, with over half the pupils maintaining that they were learning more than in school and a quarter saying that their personal problems were now being attended to more sympathetically. None the less, this report and other research literature exposed a number of concerns which, between them, cast serious doubts on the ability of off-site units to make a major contribution to the general problem of disaffection in school.

One view was that the schools could do more to pre-empt the circumstances which gave rise to pupil referrals to off-site units. Following his interviews with secondary pupils attending four units in one Midlands authority, Lloyd-Smith (1984) concluded that the home experiences suffered by the majority of those youngsters made them especially vulnerable to a particular type of 'intolerant hyper-critical teacher who is content when dealing with able, conforming and well-motivated children but has little desire or ability to appreciate the personal problems of pupils' (p.95). This view was based largely on descriptions of ex-grammar school teachers who found themselves, for the first time in their careers, teaching low-ability pupils and mixed-ability classes. Lloyd-Smith concluded that whilst a minority of referred pupils did need special placement, the majority,

> could have survived in conventional situations if their problems had been sensitively recognized and the schools had been able to respond flexibly to their needs. Disruption in schools is a problem which could be diminished dramatically if the principle of prevention rather than cure were to guide the schools' responses to it. (p.97).

In a similar vein, Basini (1981) concluded from his study of units set up by the now-defunct Inner London Education Authority that heads had welcomed units as a way of reducing suspensions, but that,

> the whole premise upon which the school support units for disruptive pupils have been established is wrong and misconceived. There is little doubt that such intervention programmes are only looking at the symptoms and not the deep underlying social causes of the problems in schools.... 'Disruptive behaviour' is as likely to be generated by the schools as constituted by ... the pupils. (p.204)

Similar observations were made by Galloway and his colleagues (1982) after investigations in Sheffield and by McManus (1987) after a study in Leeds. Galloway concluded that:

> a pupil's chances of being excluded or suspended are influenced as much, and probably more, by which school he happens to attend, as by any stress in his family or any constitutional factors in the pupil himself. (p.33)

A related issue here is the seemingly random nature of referrals, a point brought out by McDermott (1984) who also criticized the way pupils' reports often resorted to generalized labelling without being specific about the details of incidents which were causing concern.

Embedded in much criticism was the perception that off-site units had been established mainly for negative reasons, that is, to spare mainstream staff the responsibility of dealing with unwanted pupils with whom they could not cope and whose behaviour was damaging the educational chances of other pupils. As much was admitted in the generally favourable comments contained in the Mortimore *et al.* (1983) study of London units mentioned above. Although 'very impressed' by the units surveyed and by teachers who 'enabled pupils with a history of failure and unhappiness to achieve success', the researchers recognized that 'off-site units can provide a dumping ground for difficult pupils and schools can be spared the need to take responsibility for disruptive behaviour' (p.135).

In another report of alternative provision in London (ILEA, 1985), the development of behavioural units was seen as a consequence of the 'undertaker syndrome – get rid of the body at any cost' (para. 2.4). Galloway *et al.* (1982) took a similar view, suggesting from their experience in Sheffield that removal from mainstream classrooms was less for the good of the pupils taken away than for those left behind. Whitty (1984) likewise observed that:

> the sense of urgency evident in many proposals produced by local authorities arose from the needs of the mainstream schools rather than the educational needs of the pupils extracted from them. (p.139)

Another kind of problem concerned the breadth and quality of curriculum opportunities to which pupils in segregated units had access. Few, if any, off-site establishments could provide the range of specialist teaching and resources available in mainstream schools. The bulk of work frequently concentrated on attainment in basic English and mathematics. Given the fact that, for many referred pupils, their disruptive behaviour was associated with their lack of attainment in basic skills, such focus was appropriate enough; but it did not compensate for the absence of a balanced curriculum. Increasingly, units addressed this problem by forging links with ordinary schools – or, often more appropriately, with FE colleges where there was now much greater provision for students with special needs.

Critics also pointed to the mismatch between the stated objectives of reintegration and the reality of the situation. One national survey (Ling *et al.*, 1985) revealed that only 35 per cent of pupils in units returned to their original school – a not surprising state of affairs given teachers' natural reluctance to have referred pupils back in their classes (McDermott, 1984). Moreover, once readmitted to school, the behaviour problems would often reappear: in one survey covering two Northern counties (Daines, 1981), this happened in six out of very ten cases within a period of six to seven weeks. Such regression lends support to the argument that the original unacceptable behaviour was often a response to alienating conditions in the school. Off-site provision has also been shown to be an ineffective measure in reducing the number of exclusions from school (Galloway et al., 1982).

Lastly, off-site units proved to be very expensive, largely because of the high ratio of staff to pupils – a state of affairs which led Topping (1983) to conclude that they were 'strictly luxury class' in terms of cost-effectiveness. This is akin to the point made recently in a report by the Audit Commission and HMI (1992), that £53 million could have been saved in 1990/91 if the money for special schools had been reinvested to cater for special needs in mainstream schools. Today, it is estimated that a pupil in a special unit costs £5,000 a year – and that is without access to the full National Curriculum – compared to £2,000 in a mainstream school (TES, 19 March 1993). An important consideration here is that if restricted resources are directed towards a limited number of places in units, then large numbers of unreferred pupils who also present behaviour problems are effectively denied support.

The integrationist philosophy of the Warnock Report on special educational needs (DES, 1978) and the 1981 Education Act marked the beginning of the 'writing on the wall' for the eccentric 'rag bag' of provision for those pupils who had begun to be officially categorized as 'disruptive and disaffected'. Some presumed that the new procedures for drawing up formal statements of need would stem the flow of 14–16-year olds who often had been transferred to off-site provision with minimal consultation between professionals. However, because these units were not officially 'schools', there was no need for a statement. In any case, many pupils were referred to units so late in their school career that there was simply no time to complete the lengthy referral procedures. None the less, there were some pupils who were transferred to off-site units on the basis of a statement of SEN which had recommended such a placement, and this gave unit staff renewed confidence in the value of what they were providing.

Supporting the integrationist approach, the Elton Committee (whose report received immediate ministerial endorsement) exhorted schools to 'do all in their power to retain and educate all the pupils on their roll on-site' (DES, 1989, para, 6.39). True, members of the Elton team were realistic enough to recognize the need for some alternative 'breathing space' provision for pupils who 'reach a stage at which they cannot constructively be educated in ordinary schools' (para, 6.46). They also pointed to the damage which local authorities could inflict on staff morale by insisting on the readmission of excluded pupils against the judgement of the head and governors. None the less, having considered the research evidence, the Committee was emphatic in its recommendation that local authorities should maintain only a minimum of placement outside mainstream provision. The central thrust of local policy, it was argued, should be the development of adequately resourced support teams performing the dual role of working with teachers in ordinary schools and running off-site units for a strictly limited number of pupils. This latter responsibility was seen to be important in facilitating communication between units and schools. Furthermore, off-site programmes were envisaged as being essentially short-term and aimed at achieving early reintegration in mainstream provision (if necessary with extra support specified in a formal statement of special need).

Although the demise of the off-site unit can be explained in part as a response to the arguments of the integrationist special needs movement, the critical findings of research studies and the recommendations contained in the Elton Report, it is undoubtedly the National Curriculum and administrative provisions of the Education Reform Act 1988 that have had the most impact. Although there is provision for exemption in exceptional cases, the National Curriculum is essentially for all pupils, regardless of their standards of behaviour. Yet off-site units by themselves cannot possibly meet the range of resource requirements for Key Stage 4. In an earlier study of off-site units which one of us conducted (Lovey, 1991), all the teachers interviewed expressed concern about their inability to deliver the National Curriculum within the existing staffing resources, the demand for a foreign language posing the greatest threat. However, there was also anxiety about the impact of the National Curriculum on disaffected Key Stage 4 pupils. Many examples were given of individuals who would cease to attend their unit if they were forced to enter for examinations in those subjects that they had hated in mainstream school. Since assessment is an essential part of the National Curriculum, and since the assessment demands are becoming more stringent (eg, in terms of curriculum breadth and the balance between course work and written papers), schools and local authorities need to have clear policies to support pupils whose weak prospects of success presage behavioural problems or truancy. The predicaments faced by teachers of Year 10/11 disaffected pupils are echoed in the comments of Lowe (1988):

> When a young person moves along that fatalistic path which ensures that he fails to achieve success, he receives very strong messages from significant people in his environment that he is a failure. He then internalises this negative picture and we are left with a sad, despondent underfunctioning youngster. (p.51)

The other big factor is this context which arises from the 1988 Act has been the radical reorganization of school funding, particularly the depletion of money now available for behavioural support. The introduction of the Local Management of Schools (LMS) initiative, by which the greater part of funding now goes directly to schools, has meant that a smaller proportion is left for centrally-provided support services. Pressures on resources have been compounded by the arrangement in most authorities whereby pupils in units outside mainstream provision have been 'double-funded', once in their original school and again in the unit, while some authorities have had their central funds reduced still more through schools opting out of local control.

New Directions in Provision for Disaffected Pupils

Although most literature concerning the education of disaffected 14–16-year-olds is critical of both the education available in the units and the system which makes the units necessary, there is in most sources (including, as we have seen, the Elton Report) a recognition of the fact that without this provision some young people in Key Stage 4 will slip through the educational net altogether.

In its White Paper *Choice and Diversity* (DfE, 1992), the Government recommended that local authorities 'should be placed under a duty to provide education otherwise than at school where necessary to meet a pupil's needs' (para. 5.13). The nature of the envisaged provision was left obscure but, as we go to press in the spring of 1993, the Government has announced its intention to introduce a new clause in the Education Bill which will oblige LEAs to run special institutions for excluded pupils (*TES*, 19 March 1993). This could turn out to be an essentially reactive kind of solution to a problem which, as shown earlier, is judged by the critics to have arisen largely as a reponse to Government marketplace policies; and, besides doing nothing to address the sources of the difficulty, setting up special units is likely to be a very costly provision, as we have seen. However, much will depend on the scope and quality of the provision and whether the units will be an integral part of a continuum of support which includes outreach services in mainstream schools.

Off-site provision must now be tackled in a much more circumspect manner, meeting a range of stringent educational and administrative criteria. This can be illustrated in a brief description of the demanding tasks of those planning a new initiative in the London borough where one of us had had charge of an old-style off-site unit. This was to develop provision which:

- does not remove from schools the responsibility for changing the curriculum to match learning and behavioural needs;

- does not encourage those referred to see themselves as a marginalized sub-group;

- offers individual programmes according to individual needs;

- builds the self-esteem of the pupils involved;

- gives access to the National Curriculum at Key Stage 4;

- gives realistic preparation and guidance for the world of work;

- provides preparation for parenthood;

- introduces young people to enriching ways of using their leisure time;

- does not make mainstream teachers feel de-skilled;

- is cost-effective;

- has enough versatility and diversification in staffing for resources to be used in different ways as the support service develops.

In the next chapter we describe how we carried out an investigation to assess the extent to which these kinds of directions were general across the country and how far the developments in in-school support still need to be supplemented by some kind of off-site provision.

CHAPTER 2

How the Study was Conducted

Aims of the Investigation

In the previous chapter we suggested that the demise of the off-site unit is due to a combination of circumstances – part-educational, part-administrative and part-financial – which make referrals to segregated institutions increasingly problematic. Our decision to investigate the directions in which local authority support services are now moving with respect to provision for disaffected 14–16-year-olds was therefore set against the background of several factors:

- a considerable body of work in the early 1980s which criticized the workings of off-site units, their cost-effectiveness and their underlying rationale;

- the integrationist movement and policies in special educational needs stemming from the Warnock Report and 1981 Education Act;

- the recommendations of the Elton Committee which saw only a limited, if necessary, place for off-site provision and a greater emphasis on pro-active policies within ordinary schools;

- the more recent political pressures arising from the 1988 Education Reform Act, particularly those relating to the National Curriculum, Local Management of Schools and policies for schools to opt-out of LEA control and receive grant-maintained status.

The circumstances in which the present study was undertaken were not only those of radical educational and administrative change; they were also ones of emotional upheaval for many unit staff. Teachers in units that were closing or being reorganized were often very distressed at what was happening. Working in a unit is a fairly isolated activity, demanding skills and approaches to class teaching which are quite different to those found in most ordinary schools. For staff who had been away from mainstream education for four years or more, there was the added problem that they were not in the position to apply for posts which required experience with the new GCSE. The changed funding arrangements for schools, together with the effects of deepening recession, also contributed to the uncertain prospects for unit staff and the possible need for considerable retraining. These teachers were relieved to find official recognition of their skills in the Elton Report (DES, 1989) and, reassuringly, many have since become fulfilled and successful in their new role as support teachers in ordinary schools. All this suggested that, while so many unit staff were going through the same process of change, the opportunity should be taken to collect information so that others could benefit from what had sometimes been quite a traumatic experience for those who are now happily resettled.

We were also aware of many teams of workers having meetings about their proposed changes, and debating the practicalities of possible strategies without the knowledge of experience elsewhere. Yet, as we were to find, a team just a few miles away could have been through this process and, after a number of time-consuming and costly false starts, now had effective provision in place. Whilst the collection and circulation of information like this cannot totally replace the planning process necessary for a team to change direction, our view is that it can save both time and money by providing a base to work on in order to implement a new service suited to local conditions and needs.

Our study therefore had three central purposes:

- to examine, across the country, just what is happening in the current situation to support the small number of Year 11 pupils for whom mainstream school has ceased to be a realistic option

- to see what could be learnt from authorities in their post-Warnock/Elton initiatives by examining staff perceptions of the activities they organize in off-site support projects

- to consider how the more successful off-site activities and practices might be adapted for ordinary schools.

The Design of the Investigation

Our investigation was conducted during the period between the autumn of 1991 and the summer of 1992. It involved three elements:

1.　A general questionnaire which was sent to 107 local authorities in England, that is all except the Scilly Isles (which has only one secondary school) and the City of London (whose responsibility for education extends to just one primary school).

2.　A follow-up questionnaire which was sent to 40 authorities whose response to the first questionnaire had suggested that they were operating special initiatives for disaffected pupils in Year 11.

3.　Visits to selected projects and interviews with the staff to acquire more detailed information about provision for excluded pupils or others referred for behavioural reasons.

1. The National Survey

The initial survey of local authority provision was designed to find out the following:

- how many off-site units were currently maintained by the authority;

- how many of these were for Years 10 and 11 only;

- whether the pupils in the units remained on the school rolls;

- whether the pupils had access to work experience and/or to FE college facilities;

- whether the pupils returned to school for some lessons;

- the number of pupils receiving special provision because of their behavioural needs;

- whether off-site units had been or were being replaced by provision aimed at retaining pupils in mainstream education and, specifically, whether the authority operated behavioural 'outreach' services for its primary and/or secondary schools;

- how pupils were referred to any of these services.

Space was left for respondents to add further information and comments.

Completed questionnaires were returned from 65, or 61 per cent, of authorities, with a further three apologizing for not having the staff to attend to our inquiry. The questionnaires had been addressed to the head of special support services, but the usefulness of the information supplied was dependent on who had undertaken to answer the questions. The most detailed replies came from people who were directly concerned with the day-to-day work of special projects and centres. Some returns were evidently completed by hard-pressed officers who were able to submit only very general information and who – as it later transpired – sometimes seemed unaware of the scope of provision in their own area. For instance, two of the most innovative off-site projects that we found were not mentioned in the LEA returns but brought to our attention 'as a result of conversations with teachers in nearby authorities. Conversely, some officials could admit to be struggling for ideas to implement while being singularly unaware of effective provision in adjoining authorities. There is thus a high possibility that other interesting projects have not been brought to our notice. All this points to the danger in survey research of assuming that information contained in questionnaire responses tells the whole story: clearly, an efficient 'grapevine' is essential!

2. The Follow-up Questionnaire

The 40 authorities who were asked to complete a further questionnaire were chosen on the basis of one of two criteria:

- they did not rely on support work within units alone, but had a *continuum of special provision* involving both mainstream schools and off-site institutions;

- they had a particularly *effective Year 11 initiative* in either a mainstream or off-site setting.

The objective was to identify the strategies which those responsible for support projects and off-site units judged to be particularly effective in engaging the interest and commitment of referred, disaffected pupils in the latter stages of Key Stage 4. This was attempted by presenting respondents with 21 statements, each assigned to one of three categories. These focused on:

- work experience and careers;

- access to FE colleges; and

- the curriculum and activities organized in special units.

Respondents were asked to rank each statement on a scale from 1 (true) to 5 (untrue). Where a statement did not apply to the respondent's situation, the instructions were to make no judgement but to enter '0'. In addition, space was given for respondents to describe their projects and to add further comments. Many respondents took advantage of this facility, not only supplying further information in the space provided on the questionnaire but also sending us brochures and newsletters about their projects. They seemed to take much pride in what they were doing and were eager to share their experiences with us. Of the 40 questionnaires distributed, 31 were completed and returned.

Work experience was selected as one of the three areas of inquiry because of its obvious relevance to school-leavers as well as the entitlement of all children to it. The six statements in this section of the questionnaire were taken from comments made by teachers in mainstream schools at a course on work experience organized by CRAC at Cambridge in 1991 and the aims of work experience given in a DES publication (1990).

Attendance at the local FE college was the focus of a second set of statements since, in earlier surveys, teachers in charge of units have usually referred to this as a possible resource. Our concern was the extent to which work in FE was likely to be successful, what factors might influence its success and whether it remained a viable proposition in localities where there had been a shift towards individual colleges controlling their own budgets.

The last section, consisting of nine statements, related to certain activities that had traditionally been offered in off-site units and of which many of those replying to our first questionnaire had written in defence. The supposition was that, if the activities did turn out to be of special benefit to the unit clientele, then they might equally be important in improving teacher-pupil relationships in ordinary schools. The activities cited – club-type sessions (such as table-tennis and listening to music), personal and social education, basic mathematics and English, and counselling – were therefore those which we assumed could be transferred to mainstream education, albeit with some slight adaptation and additional staffing.

The items in the sections relating to FE and special activities were derived from responses to our national survey together with the experience of one of us in running an off-site unit and conducting a small-scale study two years earlier (Lovey, 1991).

The responses for each item were processed by noting the distribution of the ratings and their mean. In general, a mean below 2.5 and a bias towards '1' and '2' ratings were taken to reflect general agreement with the statement. Conversely, statements with a mean above 3.5 and which were mostly endorsed as '4' or '5' were assumed to reflect general disagreement. Account was also taken of the strength of agreement or disagreement by noting the degree to which respondents used the outer ratings. Where ratings tended to cluster around '3', it was assumed that the statement attracted a neutral judgement, while ratings spread fairly evenly across the continuum were taken to mean that consensus was lacking.

3. Visits and Interviews

As a result of the information supplied in the returns to the follow-up questionnaire, visits were made to 11 institutions – project centres, off-site units and FE colleges – to study the provision there in more detail. The places visited were chosen because of their special interest and apparent effectiveness in giving positive support to referred pupils. Although we appreciate that the thrust of development in support strategies is now within mainstream schools, we wanted to judge whether some of the particularly successful practices in off-site settings should be retained as special provision, supplementary to mainstream support, or whether they could be incorporated into ordinary school settings. Everywhere, staff were justifiably proud of their achievements and anxious to share them with us. They were also invariably welcoming and eager to prolong the visit as much as possible.

At each visit the same list of questions was asked, and interviews were recorded where permission was granted. The following topics were covered:

- aims of the provision;

- the extent to which aims were fulfilled, and reasons for any non-fulfilment;

- how pupils are selected;

- funding arrangements and difficulties;

- the impact of Key Stage 4 on the curriculum;

- exclusion rates and their implications for provision;

- work experience – whether it meets its stated aims and comes up to pupils' expectations;

- the relative merits of continuous block and part-time placements;

- the proportion of leavers finding employment within three months of leaving;

- pupils' interest in access to FE and proceeding to FE after leaving.

The information derived from our visits was updated in September 1992 when we invited the heads of some of the institutions visited in this survey, and of others, to address a conference at the Roehampton Institute called 'Key Stage 4 – A New Beginning?'.

We give an account of our findings in the next four chapters. Those from the national survey are given in the next chapter, while those derived from the follow-up questionnaire, the visits and interviews are reported in Chapters 4, 5 and 6.

CHAPTER 3

Support Provision in Year 11:
Bins or Bridges?

Our first task, as explained in the previous chapter, was to ascertain the range of provision that local authorities were currently making for Year 11 pupils who had been excluded from school or referred for special support because of behaviour problems. The findings in this chapter are based on returns made from 65 of the 107 English authorities to whom we sent a questionnaire (see last chapter). This represents an overall response rate of 61 per cent. Additionally, three LEAs sent back uncompleted questionnaires with apologies for not having the staff to attend to the items.

There was little variation in the proportion of returns from the counties, the metropolitan authorities of the North and Midlands, and the Greater London boroughs. However, within London the response rate was somewhat higher among the outer boroughs and lower among the inner boroughs (formerly the ILEA).

Support Systems

In Chapter 1, we outlined the main types of support provision which LEAs may make for Year 11 pupils with behaviour problems. The two main facilities are off-site units outside mainstream provision and 'outreach' teams that support pupils in ordinary schools and advise teachers. Although pupils with EBD are sometimes placed in special schools, this is usually before pupils reach Year 11.

Table 3.1 shows the extent to which education authorities offer off-site support in special units and/or in-school support through an outreach service. Overall, off-site units are provided in just over eight out of ten authorities which made a return. Outreach services are also provided in this proportion of authorities, demonstrating that their development has moved apace since the Elton survey in the 1980s (DES, 1989).

Table 3.1 Authorities with off-site and outreach support services

Support facility	Gr. London (N=21)	Metropol. (N=20)	County (N=24)	All (N=65)
		Number of authorities		
Off-site provision only	1	0	8	9
Combined off-site and outreach provision	17	13	14	44
Outreach only	3	4	1	8
Neither facility	0	3	1	4

However, the table also suggests contrasting policies between the three categories of authority as regards the emphasis given to off-site and outreach provision. The counties seem to rely more on supporting pupils in off-site units (all but two counties had this facility) than by using outreach teams in ordinary schools, a service which has yet to be developed in one-third of these authorities. Among the metropolitan authorities, the reverse is the case, one-third having no off-site provision and no authority relying exclusively on this kind of support alone. In Greater London, however, the policy seems to be based more on combinations of in-school and off-site p~vision, eight out of ten boroughs offering a continuum of support involving both kinds of facility compared with rather less than one-third in the counties and metropolitan authorities. In general, it would appear that the demise of the off-site unit is most pronounced in urban areas of the Midlands and North, whilst attempts to keep pupils in school by giving pupils support through outreach services are more often found in these authorities and the Greater London area than in the counties.

Among those authorities which give special support in off-site units alone, we found little evidence of changing policy towards in-school support. Comments on the returns suggested that only two of the nine authorities concerned had plans for the addition of outreach services within the ordinary schools. On the other hand, among the authorities with combined outreach and unit provision, several had plans to shift resources more into the former, while some authorities commented that numbers in units had declined with the success of greater in-school support and were used more as a part-time tutorial facility than for pupils' full-time education.

Turning now to the numbers of off-site units maintained by authorities, the figures in Table 3.2 clearly demonstrate a decline since the 1980 survey by the Advisory Centre for Education (ACE). At that time there were 386 units in the 50 per cent of UK authorities which made a return, 226 units being in the Inner London Education Authority alone. In contrast, the present survey revealed a total of just 108 units in the 61 per cent sample of English authorities. The table also reveals that most authorities with off-site provision maintain just one or two units (more often two in Greater London), although 11 have between three and five units, and one (a Southern county) has as many as eight. Differences in the numbers of units between authorities is not a simple function of differences in pupil numbers and type of area: for instance, another Southern county with a higher secondary population has only two units.

Table 3.2 Authorities maintaining off-site units

| Number of off-site units | Number of authorities | | | |
	Gr. London (N=21)	Metropol. (N=20)	County (N=24)	All (N=65)
0	3	7	2	12
1	5	8	9	22
2	11	2	6	19
3	1	2	3	6
4	1	1	1	3
5	–	–	2	2
6	–	–	–	–
7	–	–	–	–
8	–	–	1	1
Number of authorities with off-site units	18	13	22	53
Total number of units	34	22	52	108

We also asked authorities to say how many Year 11 pupils were receiving special provision because of their behavioural needs. Few respondents provided an answer to this question, revealing perhaps that such statistics are not uniformly kept. However, among those that did reply, the number of pupils usually ranged between 10 and 15, though in three large metropolitan authorities it was a high as 55, 150 and 300.

When pupils are referred to off-site units, the feeder school legally retains responsibility for their education unless they have been permanently excluded. From our data it appears that schools did keep unit pupils on their rolls in most (38) of the 53 authorities with units, although nine did not, while six had no policy or did not answer the question. However, this also means that in the great majority of cases pupils in units are double-funded, once in school and again in the unit. Clearly it is the schools and their non-referred pupils which are benefiting from this arrangement.

In view of criticisms which have often been made about the restricted curriculum opportunities in off-site provision, we asked each authority whether it was the practice for unit pupils to return to schools for some lessons. No authority seems to have a clear policy about this unless the off-site placement is an integral part of a continuum of provision. In other cases, the decision is left to teachers in schools and units to negotiate if they so wish.

Work Experience and Access to FE Colleges

For many years, work experience has been recognized as important for disaffected Year 11 pupils. Its supporters argue that not only does it provide the opportunity for participants to become employable and ready for the world of work, it can also contribute towards the pupils' growth in self-awareness, self-confidence and independence. FE too is often considered to offer new opportunities for pupils to realize success. As post-16 qualifications become more important in our society, and as we develop closer links with Europe where post-school training and education is more the rule, the ability of Year 11 school-leavers to sustain courses in further education is become increasingly important.

Table 3.3 shows the number of authorities offering work experience and FE courses to Year 11 pupils receiving special support in both off-site units and ordinary schools. All but four authorities offer work experience, and almost three-quarters provide access to FE in addition to this (though this does not mean that places are in fact found, or can be afforded, for all those who want them). Hardly any authorities give

Table 3.3 Authorities offering work experience and FE courses to pupils in behaviour support projects

Facility	Gr. London (N=21)	Metropol. (N=20)	County (N=24)	All (N=65)
Work experience only	5	5	5	15
Work experience and access to FE	16	15	15	46
Access to FE only	0	0	2	2
Neither facility	0	0	2	2

access to FE without also providing the opportunity for work experience. One authority without an off-site unit has set up a vocational college for 14 – 19-year-olds to which Year 11 pupils with behavioural problems can be referred. This exciting development, which offers a combination of curriculum studies, work experience and FE-type training, is described in some detail in Chapter 5.

Unfortunately, as comments on the questionnaire reveal, work experience placements and, even more so, FE links, are becoming harder to arrange. The present high levels of unemployment seem to deter employers offering placements to pupils who have a history of behaviour problems. As regards FE, colleges are becoming more cost-conscious with the advent of delegated budgeting and they now charge for their facilities, putting them beyond the means of many support services.

Summary

Among the 61 per cent of English authorities in the sample, the vast majority provide off-site units (mostly one or two) or outreach services, and over two-thirds provide both facilities; however among the urban authorities there is a greater tendency than in counties to shift resources into outreach provision, thus keeping pupils in need of special support in ordinary schools. In most, but not all, authorities, unit pupils are retained on their school roll, but a few authorities have no policy about this. Whether unit pupils return to schools for some lessons is left to personal negotiation except in situations where there is a continuum of provision involving both in-school and off-site support. Work experience is almost always offered to Year 11 pupils receiving support, and FE very often too, though in both cases places are becoming harder to arrange.

CHAPTER 4

Work Experience

As described in Chapter 2, a follow-up questionnaire was sent to selected personnel in 40 authorities and returned by 31 respondents. Those who had responsibility for off-site units and other special provision for the support of disaffected pupils in Year 11 were invited to make judgements with respect to a number of statements relating to three sets of activity: work experience, access to FE colleges, and certain curriculum and social activities located in off-site units. Subsequently, personal visits were made to 11 authorities, where more detailed information and staff perceptions about the three areas of activity were recorded. In this chapter, we examine the findings from the follow-up questionnaire, interviews and visits as they relate to work experience.

The Value and Popularity of Work Experience

For almost two decades, work experience has been part of the curriculum for many Year 11 pupils, and most schools have staff specially responsible for making the arrangements. All but two of the replies to our national survey (Chapter 3) stated that local authorities were prepared to extend work experience opportunities to pupils in units or within-school behaviour projects, while virtually all respondents to the follow-up questionnaire found the work experience items relevant to their local situation (see N/A column in Table 4). Teachers who have been associated with this kind of work often remark on the 'growth' that occurs in pupils during a successful work experience, and urge that the pupils participating should be recognized as young persons whose experiences should be shared and exploited with others in the group as much as possible.

As the mean rating for the second item in Table 4.1 reveals, there was general agreement with the proposition that work experience is a popular option among disaffected pupils, with only one in five respondents dissenting from this view. Moreover, most of those agreeing did so unequivocally, while only one of the dissenting respondents disagreed totally.

Table 4.1 Ratings for Work Experience

| Statement | Number of respondents (N=31) | | | | | | | |
	N/A	1	2	Rating 3	4	5	Mean	SD
Many Year 11 pupils are already working for a wage	1	3	5	7	8	7	3.37	1.30
Work experience is a popular option for this group of pupils	0	14	6	5	5	1	2.13	1.26
This group of pupils is unwilling to do work experience unless they are receiving some cash incentive	0	3	4	4	14	6	3.52	1.23
With the right employer these pupils can do very well	0	25	4	1	0	1	1.32	0.83
Work experience placements require a great commitment from the teachers	0	24	5	2	0	0	1.29	0.59
Work experience motivates pupils to come back and take advantage of the curriculum offered to school-leavers	1	2	6	15	1	6	3.10	1.16

Note: The direction of ratings is from 1 (agreement) to 5 (disagreement). Figures in the N/A column indicate the number of respondents who 'passed' on the grounds that the statement was not applicable to their particular situation.

The significance of work experience as an antidote for disaffection was generally recognized amongst those we talked to on our visits. Staff emphasized the way in which work experience not only gave pupils knowledge about production methods and daily work routines but also helped them to acquire a sense of individual responsibility and skills in teamwork. The principal of a vocational college in the North-East enthused about the importance of work experience in relation to a cohort of 14–16-year-olds who had been excluded from school and accepted for the remainder of their compulsory education:

> It's vital. The first stage is to come into college and relate to the safe adults there. The next stage is to go out and use those skills where they are not known and protected.

One of the perceived advantages of work experience according to a DES publication (1990) is that pupils return to classroom work with greater motivation to take advantage of the curriculum offered to school-leavers. However, we found no enthusiasm to endorse this belief: around half the respondents sat on the fence, with the remaining half divided almost equally between those who expressed a measure of agreement and those who disagreed (see Table 4.1, last item).

Factors Influencing Success

As we have seen, although work experience was generally perceived to be well-liked by project pupils, a third of the respondents supplied a neutral rating or expressed some degree of misgiving about its popularity (see Table 4.1, second item). One reason for this could be that it does not seem particularly relevant to those pupils who have their own part-time jobs. That some pupils clearly are already in waged employment is suggested in the ratings to the first statement in Table 4.1, though a fair number of respondents seemed unable to commit themselves on this matter. Of course, perceptions of the relevance of work experience among pupils already employed would no doubt depend upon the comparison they make between the opportunities given in their present place of work and those offered in project placements. All in all, however, the response to the statement in this item suggests that work experience, for some pupils at least, does allow insight into an area of life not previously encountered.

The factor which respondents believed was most important for ensuring success in a work experience placement is the commitment of the employers to the project arrangements. As shown in the table, there was nearly complete endorsement (mean rating = 1.3) for the suggestion that success could be assured provided there was the 'right' employer, only two respondents giving a neutral or negative rating. On the other hand, comparatively little support was forthcoming for the suggestion that successful work experience was dependent on cash incentives: fewer than a quarter of respondents indicated agreement with this view against two-thirds expressing some measure of disagreement.

Other factors perceived to be prerequisites for successful work experience emerged during the personal interviews and visits. One which was given particular emphasis was ensuring that participants were properly prepared. And, as the head of one unit emphasized, to the importance of early groundwork must be added the need for relevant post-experience activity:

In the past work experience as was not very successful, but now we spend much
more time preparing for it more thoroughly. We also use enterprise weeks as a
follow-up from this.

Two other important success factors were that the demands made on
pupils must be moderately challenging and liaison between work place
and unit secure and friendly. As one unit head in Teesdale remarked:

They either have a very good experience and do extremely well, or they fail on the
first day. They generally fail because they haven't been prepared or they are doing very
routine work. The best work experience is when the employing staff are resident in our
community or when they are well-known to us.

One of the main characteristics of work experience in many off-site
projects is the flexibility afforded for its programming. In mainstream
schools, freedom in the allocation of time-slots for placements and the
pupils' preparation is necessarily constrained by the exigencies of the
subject timetable. Work experience may therefore need to be confined to
a block placement during that part of the year when subject
commitments are least pressing. On our visits, we therefore asked
support service personnel to comment on the question of whether it is
more effective to organize work experience in a continuous block of time
or to spread it over a period by using one or two days per week.

Differing views were expressed on this issue, though the consensus
seemed to be that a flexible approach was needed since much depended
on how individuals reacted. The staff of one vocational college preferred
to start pupils off with a 'trial' block one week, followed by another after
a short gap; but the flexibility was such that pupils who could not sustain
a whole week at first could often be rescued by spending one day a week
at work with the rest of the time in college before attempting another
continuous period of experience. In contrast, a head of a unit in the
North-East preferred, as a matter of course, to organize the first work
experience placement on a part-time basis, following it later with a block
of seven days if all went well. However, another unit head in the same
region maintained that pupils were more likely to succeed in a week's or
even fortnight's experience than in single days, when staff sometimes
had to fetch pupils from home. With such individualized arrangements as
those described, success in work experience could generally be assured,
though not invariably: one 19-year-old, we were told, had never
managed a complete week and there were doubts about his
employability.

A problem for support services is how to convince non-attenders that work experience can be valuable for them. In one case involving a group of truanting pupils, the head of a support project undertook a special form of 'outreach' work, meeting the individuals on their own territory such as the steps of the town hall or by a wall at the end of a council estate. In these kinds of location, she was usually able to negotiate special activities, the most popular of which usually turned out to be work experience. Those who decided to pursue this had to commit themselves to a pre-arranged number of regular meetings with a member of the support staff to discuss possible types of placement and to receive some preparation for the choices made. There was also the expectation that everyone would continue to meet after the initial experience had been completed.

In general, it was widely believed that the value of good work experience was most of all in terms of its contribution to pupils' self-esteem. But conversely, unsuitable experience from which pupils were either expelled or absented themselves could be very damaging to pupils' feelings of worth. However, work experience was not necessarily a personal disaster for pupils who failed in the early stages. The crucial mediating factor was the quality of support given by the project staff. The principal of the vocational college in the North-East referred to earlier was one who insisted that participation in work experience could be good even for pupils who at first react badly. In these circumstances, he emphasized, the supporting role of his staff was very important, even if such in-house protection needed to be balanced by the more 'realistic' treatment of the work place:

> If they are rude and uncooperative on work experience they get thrown off it. Then the college works through with them what happened. A lot have been offered jobs from their work experience. There is a problem with the positive reinforcement they get here that some pupils get an unrealistic idea of their capabilities. It is better if someone from outside knocks the ladder out from under them as the staff are then here to pick them up again.

Respondents to the questionnaire were virtually unanimous in believing that work experience placements require great commitment from the project staff (mean rating = 1.3). During the visits, one Midlands teacher in an area of low employment was particularly concerned that, since staff needed to use a great deal of their own time in arranging placements, they should receive more recognition for this aspect of their work.

Work Experience in Project Centres

In spite of the general belief that work experience is popular and likely to be successful, the prevailing view in the authorities we visited was that the present employment situation made it more difficult to find suitable placements for Year 11 pupils. It was also pointed out that certain kinds of work experience, though desirable in principle, were not practicable propositions. The main example cited here was the construction industry in which placements were difficult to arrange because of the necessary rigid safety requirements.

However, the personnel we interviewed did not rely on work off-site in order to arrange suitable experiences. Because of problems in organizing more than one placement for each pupil, work-related activities were often carried out in the project centre itself. Training managers from local industry might organize one- or two-day courses which included interactive games, or teachers themselves might set up real or simulated business enterprises with groups of pupils who would take on various roles in rotation. Increasingly, on-site work experience can be given added value if the skills can be listed and assessed as NVQs, with accreditation from a recognized examination board.

In two projects we visited, on-site work experience was found to be especially important for those young people who insisted on adopting extreme modes of dress and hairstyle, which made it difficult to persuade employers to accept them in the workplace. In these cases, efforts to organize enterprises on-site proved to be most rewarding. An example of a particularly effective arrangement was found in a unit which the organizers had opted to accommodate on an industrial site rather than in an old school building. The unit has an integral pottery factory, producing a range of mugs and tankards, individualized with ceramic transfers. Here pupils acquire skills in all the stages of production, while also learning the importance of individual responsibility and teamwork through having to meet targets and deadlines. Opportunity is afforded not only for pupils to achieve success in 15 identified competencies but also to make enough profit to pay for their annual ski-trip! Part of the day is devoted to a more conventional curriculum so that pupils are not restricted in their post-16 options. There is also opportunity for sport and recreational activities.

In another centre, the support staff had set up a garden furniture workshop and working farm. As well as providing work experience internally, the skills involved in both these enterprises had been identified and listed, and NVQs were offered to those successful in meeting the targets.

Summary

Work experience is generally, but not invariably, perceived as popular for pupils in support projects. Not only is it seen as teaching participants specific work skills, but is also helps to enhance self-esteem and feelings of self-confidence. Experience located in a project centre can also make a very important contribution to pupils' personal development and employability, especially if the skills acquired can contribute to NVQs.

The two most important factors influencing success in work experience appear to be (1) the commitment of the employer to the value of work experience for this group of pupils, and (2) time set aside by project staff for thorough preparation and follow-up. Other factors which make for success involve making sure that: the tasks are not simply routine but offer a degree of challenge; there is effective liaison with workplace staff (better still if the latter are locally resident and known personally to project personnel); the timing of placements is flexible enough to meet individual needs; in-house support is given to pupils at risk of failing; and the project staff are willing to put a lot of effort outside of school hours into fixing-up suitable arrangements.

CHAPTER 5

Access to Further Education

The second issue which we investigated in the follow-up questionnaire and visits was the extent to which access to FE was perceived to be valuable and what factors were likely to maximize its success. As we reported in Chapter 2, roughly four-fifths of local authorities reported to us that they have use of FE facilities for Key Stage 4 pupils who had been referred because of behaviour problems; and, as the first column in Table 5.1 reveals, all but a few of the respondents to our follow-up questionnaire felt that the items on FE were applicable to their local situation.

Factors Influencing Success in FE Links

Table 5.1 shows that our respondents gave moderate support for the view that pupils who are unsuccessful at school will often succeed on a suitable college course. There was no outright disagreement with this view, though a fair number reserved judgement.

Turning now to the reasons why success in FE courses may or may not be experienced by pupils in special support projects, there was moderate support for two of the three factors suggested in the questionnaire items. First of all, it would seem that the presence of other pupils from the same project group is a determining factor in at least some cases. Respondents were markedly more likely to agree that pupils work better on a course if they are the only one of their group on roll than to agree that pupils work best when they attend with other support group members (means = 2.41 v. 3.70). However, during the course of our visits, we also found an effective arrangement whereby *all* participants were group members. The provision here involved special tailor-made programmes for pupils in three off-site units, who pooled resources to support a range of courses at a local college. Although each

Table 5.1 Ratings for links with FE

| Statement | Number of respondents (N=31) | | | | | | | |
	N/A	1	2	3	4	5	Mean	SD
Pupils who have not succeeded in school often succeed in a suitable college course	2	5	13	9	2	0	2.28	0.84
Pupils succeed best if they are the only one of their group in a particular college course	4	8	8	6	2	3	2.41	1.31
Pupils succeed best if they are on a college course with a number of others from the same project	4	1	4	5	9	8	3.70	1.17
EBD pupils can benefit from sharing in the courses arranged for MLD pupils	4	3	1	7	7	9	3.67	1.30
Pupils will stick at a course if they know they will receive a qualification at the end	0	2	12	11	5	1	2.71	0.94
Since Local Management of Colleges there have been financial problems in sending Year 11 pupils to college	5	16	4	1	2	3	1.92	1.44

Note: The direction of ratings is from 1 (agreement) to 5 (disagreement). Figures in the N/A column indicate the number of respondents who 'passed' on the grounds that the statement was not applicable to their particular situation.

unit had only 24-30 pupils, the three combined had sufficient numbers to make a choice of courses possible.

A second factor which appeared to influence the success of FE links was the nature of the target students for which the course had been designed. Pupils in support projects are sometimes given places on courses which are designed primarily for individuals with mild learning difficulties (MLD). As Table 5.1 shows, the statement that pupils with emotional and behavioural difficulties (EBD) can benefit from sharing in courses arranged for pupils with MLD attracted mainly neutral and negative ratings (mean = 3.70). The reasons for this became plain during discussions on our visits: although the academic demands made in these courses were well-matched to the abilities of the project pupils, many resented being associated with programmes that they identified as meant really for 'thickies'. This was especially the case where there were students with Downs Syndrome or other recognizable 'handicapping' features.

The other factor investigated was the possibility that success depends on the prospects of receiving a qualification at the end of the course. However, the bunching of ratings around '2' and '3' for the item relating to this suggestion demonstrates no clear consensus among respondents.

The Impact of Delegated Financial Management

As more FE colleges now move to delegated management and then to self-governing status, we were interested to know whether the shift towards local budget control was having any effect on access to FE for disaffected pupils. The main problem, we had heard, was that funding problems for colleges under delegated management structures have led to fees being charged for link courses. Consistent with this view, the ratings in Table 5.1 demonstrate strong endorsement for the statement that 'since Local Management of Colleges there have been financial problems in sending Year 11 pupils to college'. It is sad that one of the most potentially effective resources for disaffected pupils is now suffering from the budgetary effects of the local management initiative so that support projects can sometimes not afford to send their pupils to college. Presumably the situation will be perpetuated as FE colleges move out of council control altogether.

Two Examples of Special College Provision

In the rest of this chapter, we give accounts from our visits of two college arrangements which seemed unusually effective. One of these was in a vocational college for 14 – 19-year-olds rather than in FE, and the other was a special course organized jointly by FE and support service staff.

A Vocational College for 14 – 19 -year-olds

In one North-Eastern authority, there are no off-site units since all excluded pupils are offered a place in a vocational college for 150 14 – 19-year-olds with special educational needs. Some of the students here have formal statements of need, but the large majority have not. Of those who are statemented, most have a physical disability such as deafness, blindness, or cerebral palsy, while some have multiple handicap caused by pre-natal exposure to rubella. Those without statements are students who, in many other authorities, would have been referred to off-site units. All those transferring from ordinary schools (some to use the college as a sixth form facility) must have the agreement of the head, the school psychologist, the parents and the student. However, most have already been excluded from mainstream education anyway, and the only alternative provision for them would be individual ('home') tuition.

Each student is admitted for an initial six-week assessment period. During this time they are given a great deal of individual support and encouragement, but expected to keep the college rules. Towards the end of this period, the student decides whether to become a full member of the college or not. In the four years during which the college has been open, no student has been excluded, though 12 have failed to attend, or have decided not to continue, or were not accepted in the first place because they were considered too potentially disruptive for this kind of provision. All the same, a number of students in the college had a record of delinquency or disruption at school, and some of these had failed in behavioural regimes and therapeutic settings. One of the boys had appeared on television during the week of the Meadowell Estate riots and had expressed his admiration of really good 'ram-raiders': he himself had only been into 'TWOCking' (taking without owner's consent).

The aims of the college, as stated to us, were simple: to make students more 'jobworthy' by helping them internalize their strengths and gradually become less dependent on external controls. The only sanction is withdrawal from the curriculum, while good behaviour is constantly reinforced. Not surprisingly, the college is seen by the local authority as a near-panacea for adolescents with almost every kind of problem.

There is a core curriculum which is modular and thematic, with assessment at the end of each module. Apart from this, the majority of courses are vocationally-directed. The college has its own farm and is the only place in the city teaching GCSE horticulture. One boy whom we interviewed there had recently completed his six-week assessment period and was enjoying work in one of the farm buildings. He had already acquired a mass of 'hands-on' knowledge: the characteristics of different manure mixes, the significance of using animal manure for vegetables and flowers, why calcium was added to goat's feed, how to spin fleeces from the flock of sheet kept in the college grounds. Other forms of work experience available include a mini-business entailing making and selling garden furniture. Additionally, for one or two weeks every half term the college suspends the timetable for a range of mini-enterprises for which students have to clock in and out. There are projects in upholstery, furniture restoration (run by a deaf mute instructor, so all participants must learn sign language), car maintenance, home economics, refurbishing apartments bought through a charity and selling them at a profit, selling fresh produce from the farm or using the farm's ingredients to prepare and sell baked products. Everybody who runs an enterprise has a trading account, and students are totally involved in keeping account books, organizing publicity for sales, writing letters, and a range of other business tasks. However, some enterprises involve voluntary work – perhaps cutting old people's hedges, for example, or typing out a carol sheet in Braille for a Christmas service attended by blind people. At the end of every summer term, a popular 'enterprise exhibition' is held at the civic centre. Through all these various pursuits, it is not perhaps surprising that more students obtain employment on leaving college than from most schools in this area of high unemployment.

Some enterprises are supported from the usual local authority GSA funding, but other sources are used too. These include the European Social Fund, TVEI and YT funding, a charity for young people with learning difficulties, and profits from the enterprises themselves. The whole atmosphere of the college is one where all concerned are happy with each other's success in doing things, and there is a quiet courtesy between staff and students. In spite of their background of behaviour problems, the students conduct themselves in exemplary fashion, making guests feel extremely welcome and showing them round with tremendous pride. The staff are frustrated at the prospect of a National Curriculum which, if followed exactly, would provide an unacceptable straitjacket on what is now an exciting and innovative project which serves well a group of young people in one of the most notoriously deprived areas of the country. None the less, the college tries to meet the demands of Key Stage 4 by embedding most attainment targets within its courses and enterprises.

A 15-week Modular Course

In one inner-London borough, two 15-week courses, run jointly by staff from an FE college and the support service, are offered for disaffected pupils during their last term-and-a-half at school. Many of these pupils had not appeared at school for over a year and could not even be persuaded to attend individual tuition regularly. The courses, to which pupils are referred by their school or the educational social work service, are based in a small suite of college rooms set aside for the purpose. The first is for Easter leavers and begins in November, the second for summer leavers beginning in February.

The first of four component modules comprises three weeks of induction activities to allow students to learn about themselves and how to work effectively in group situations. A range of tasks are organized to build self-esteem and skills in self-evaluation. This module is followed by one week in a residential setting at an activity centre. Some pupils drop out at this point, but the majority who continue proceed to the third module, which involves a three-week block of work experience preceded by a week's preparation. An important aspect of the support given is that, if the work experience breaks down, the pupil can repeat the module at the end of the course, possibly making a fresh start in a different placement.

The last module during the remaining weeks of the course is used to prepare pupils for transition to work. There is an emphasis on personal and social education, health matters, community education and careers guidance. Debriefing from work experience and help in applying for jobs come at the end of the course, so that support might overrun the official 15 weeks.

Summary

Many support projects have access to FE courses, a facility which can offer opportunities for success to pupils who have been failing at school. The availability of a terminal qualification is not necessarily a pre-requisite for this success, but the make-up of course group membership does seem to make a difference. In general, it appears that pupils are more successful if they are the only one of their project group attending, though one successful case was found where whole groups from local support projects enrolled for special tailor-made college courses. Also, project pupils sometimes resent being members of courses designed for those with mild learning difficulties.

The two special examples described in this chapter point to ways in which FE provision can be used imaginatively and effectively to support youngsters who present behaviour problems in conventional school regimes, and suggest that in-school support alone is probably not a sufficient answer to the problem of disaffection among older secondary pupils. Unfortunately, however, funding problems under recent delegated budget initiatives are making FE provision too expensive for many support projects.

CHAPTER 6

On-site Activities in Off-site Units

The activities which are the subject of this chapter are referred to as 'on-site' since they are those that the college, centre, scheme, project or unit organizes for its own clientele in the unit building itself.

The third section of our follow-up questionnaire to selected personnel consisted of nine items which covered four aspects of on-site activity: 'club-type' sessions, personal and social education, basic work in maths and English, and counselling. As can be seen from Table 6.1, each of these areas – with the exception of PSE organized by an outside agency – was part of the support programmes familiar to almost all respondents.

Courses in Basic Maths and English

A considerable body of evidence points to an association between antisocial behaviour and learning difficulties, though the cause-effect relationship is not altogether clear (review in Docking, 1987). Concern about low levels of achievement in basic skills among school-leavers is also frequently expressed by employers, politicians and in media reports. It is therefore not surprising that the respondents to the questionnaire considered attention to basic number work, reading and writing to be generally well-received. As can be seen from Table 6.1, almost one in three respondents considered basic skills courses to be popular with both pupils and parents, especially among the latter in relation to whom this view tended to be expressed particularly strongly. At the same time, the ratings suggested virtually no strong dissension from the general feeling about the popularity of basic skills courses among pupils and parents.

Table 6.1 Ratings for on-site activities in off-site units

Statement	N/A	1	2	3	4	5	Mean	SD
				Number of respondents (N=31) Rating				
A club-type session with games, etc. is valuable in getting to understand pupils	2	13	11	1	2	2	1.93	1.19
A club-type session is a useful carrot to help keep pupils involved in school or college	2	8	8	5	5	3	2.55	1.35
Courses in PSE offered by project staff are popular with pupils	2	4	7	12	6	0	2.69	0.97
Courses in PSE offered by outside agencies are more popular with pupils	7	3	3	9	4	2	2.69	1.08
Formal teaching in PSE is a very important aspect of the project	3	6	4	9	4	5	2.93	1.39
Examination courses in basic maths and English are popular with pupils	1	8	10	5	5	2	2.43	1.25
Examination courses in basic maths and English are popular with parents of pupils	3	11	8	4	4	1	2.14	1.21
Formal arrangements for counselling individuals are an important aspect of the project	2	10	7	2	4	6	2.62	1.59
Informal counselling of individuals by project staff is an important aspect of the project	1	22	5	1	0	2	1.50	1.07

Note: The direction of ratings is from 1 (agreement) to 5 (disagreement). Figures in the N/A column indicate the number of respondents who 'passed' on the grounds that the statement was not applicable to their particular situation.

Club-type Sessions

We used this term to refer to those times when pupils sit and chat or play games such as table-tennis, snooker, monopoly or trivial pursuits, or when they watch their choice of television or video, or listen to their personal selection of music.

As the distribution of ratings for the first item in Table 6.1 reveals, all but a handful of project personnel regarded these activities as valuable in helping them to understand the pupils, and this view was frequently held strongly. At the same time, there was markedly less support for the idea that club pursuits acted as a carrot to keep pupils involved in more serious activities. In our interviews, staff emphasized the value of club activities in forging relationships between disturbed young people and 'safe' adults.

Courses in PSE

The three statements on personal and social education in the follow-up questionnaire netted more uncommitted answers than any item. No clear consensus emerged about the popularity of the courses, those run by outside agencies being no better received than those taught by the project staff. Everybody in the comments section of the questionnaire who offered some information about their curriculum mentioned also the importance of PSE. Yet the ratings for the statement which asked for opinion on this matter show no consensus of opinion, though a small minority expressed strong agreement or disagreement.

It would seem, too, that the definition of PSE as well as its popularity and value is a matter of some considerable controversy among project staff. During the interviews, many teachers maintained that their most important contribution to PSE was informal interaction with pupils and in providing a positive atmosphere rather than in organizing structured timetabled work. The comments by one teacher in charge of a unit in a London borough seem to ignore even the possibility of formal provision in this area:

> Re PSE. We find that theoretically this can be described in terms of two qualities in our unit: (i) in the sense that the ethos of our unit fosters renewed self-esteem; and (ii) in dealing with immediate issues for the group and individual.

Clearly this perspective on PSE overlaps not only with the work that staff can undertake during club activities but with the concept of counselling, which was the next topic we examined.

Counselling

There was no doubt among the questionnaire respondents that the counselling of individuals was an important activity; but, as with PSE, it was the informal rather than formal arrangements which were seen to be of particular value (means = 1.50 v. 2.62). Although more respondents that not agreed totally or partially with the statement that formal counselling was an important part of support projects, the majority was a small one and a third expressed a measure of disagreement. In contrast, almost two-thirds of respondents were in total agreement with the statement that informal counselling was important, and hardly any expressed neutrality or disagreement.

In an appended comment, one respondent maintained that unit pupils often reject what he called 'proper' counselling when given by project staff since they see this as the job of professional counsellors with special qualifications. The writer also suggested that in so far as formal counselling can provoke aggression, it would be difficult to justify its general practice in the climate of an off-site unit. At the same time, he wanted to emphasize 'the sense that counselling involves *listening*', which he saw as 'a dominating aspect of our relationships with student', adding that many ex-pupils return to 'talk', often many years after they have left the unit. In fact we witnessed a group of pupils returning to a unit to express gratitude for the help they had received because, 'there had always been someone to listen to you'. The significance for ordinary schools which the vast majority of staff attached to 'constructive listening' will be discussed in the last chapter.

Effect of Key Stage 4

It was clear from comments made in the questionnaire for the national survey, as well as those made during our visits, that unit heads were anxious about the effect which the implementation of Key Stage 4 regulations would have on club activities and time available for counselling. It will be important in the years to come for this situation to be monitored to ensure that unit staff still have the flexibility to make this kind of social provision they believe is so important for this group of pupils.

Summary

Courses in basic English and maths are generally popular with pupils and, even more so, with their parents. Among the social activities in units, there is no question that support project staff view club-type pursuits as highly important, particularly for their potential in furthering teacher-pupil understanding. As regards courses in personal and social education, there seems much division of opinions about both its popularity and value. In contrast, although there is only moderate support for formal counselling, the importance of informal counselling is widely acknowledged, particularly in so far as pupils greatly appreciate the willingness of an adult who will listen to their concerns. The effects of the National Curriculum on the scope for unit activities will need to be monitored.

CHAPTER 7

Towards Effective Provision

From the evidence we collected in the national survey, it seems that the vast majority of education authorities still provide off-site units, though more so in the London areas and the counties than in the metropolitan authorities. However, the number of off-site units is now substantially less than it was; and, of those left, many now admit pupils on a strictly part-time basis for a limited amount of time and for more specific objectives, often supplementing the provision with work experience and possibly FE.

Since the late 1980s, eight out of ten authorities (though a smaller proportion in the counties) have developed outreach services, while two out of three authorities (more in Greater London) now provide a combination of outreach and off-site support. The shift in resources from off-site to outreach provision is justified mainly on the grounds that it enables more pupils with behaviour problems to be kept in ordinary schools and thus to enjoy continued access to a full range of curriculum opportunities and resources.

In this chapter, we address three broad but interrelated issues regarding provision and support for Key Stage 4 pupils presenting major behaviour problems. These are:

1. How successful are current types of off-site provision?

2. To what extent could the best of current practice in off-site provision be provided in ordinary schools?

3. Is there still a case for some kind of off-site provision to support disaffected pupils in Year 11?

Most of the discussion which follows is based on replies to the follow-up questionnaire and visits to 11 authorities whose provision seemed particularly far-ranging or innovative, but some ideas are also drawn from evidence and views presented at a conference on disaffection in Key Stage 4, held at the Roehampton Institute in September 1992.

1. How Successful is Off-site Provision?

Although a good deal has been written about off-site units, much has described what happens in particular settings without exploring which activities seem most likely to achieve their objectives. It must be acknowledged, of course, that few units would be able to sustain strategies which were not generally working since the project pupils would simply sabotage them or stay away. None the less, it is important to identify those pursuits which are particularly effective and the conditions which make them so.

The evaluation of any educational enterprise is bound to be subjective. Even when agreement is reached on the criteria for successful achievement (often a major source of controversy), there remains the problem of determining appropriate means of assessing the extent to which the criteria have been satisfied. This is problematic enough with respect to the National Curriculum in ordinary schools. It is even more so with respect to special activities in off-site units for pupils who not only present behaviour problems but who also, for the most part, carry a history of failure or non-attendance in mainstream provision. When one then moves to identifying the *reasons* for a successful activity, there is a further difficulty: that of separating evidence relating to the effectiveness of the strategy itself from that relating to the effectiveness of the member of staff. We found that off-site units were often lucky enough to have teachers whose enthusiasm for some pursuits, perhaps outdoor activities or drama, knew no bounds and who clearly were instrumental in creating a positive ethos in the unit. In these circumstances it was difficult to know how to apportion responsibility for success between the personal characteristics of the teacher and the features of the activity itself.

A further problem in our evaluation of support project provision was that we could only make a judgement about the realization of short – and medium term – objectives. For instance, project staff might maintain that a particular kind of activity had enabled pupils who had been disruptive at school, or conspicuous in their non-attendance, to develop better relationships with adults in the unit or successfully sustain a whole week's work experience; they might also, after a longer period, express the belief that the pupils' basic attitudes towards those in authority had changed for the better or that they were successfully acquiring a range of skills necessary for the workplace. But the staff would not be able to say with confidence whether pupils would be able to maintain their more acceptable behaviour and changed attitudes after they had left the setting and protection of the support project – though here again, subjective information was sometimes available when staff cited examples of pupils who had left and with whom they had maintained contact.

We turn now to consider the success of off-site provision with respect to our main areas of focus: work experience, FE, and personal development.

Work Experience

Consistently, work experience was seen by staff to be an important issue, not only helping pupils to improve their prospects of employability but also making a major contribution to their personal growth. Although it was generally (but not invariably) popular among pupils, its success appeared to be dependent on a range of factors, some related to the workplace itself, others to the quality of support given by the project team.

As regards characteristics of the workplace, there were three factors of particular importance: (1) the employer's commitment to making the experience work; (2) the provision of tasks which were reasonably challenging and not simply routine; (3) flexibility in accommodating pupils' varying needs through making both block and part-time work available, especially if it was also possible to move less-successful pupils from one form of timing to the other.

As far as support by the project team is concerned, the following four factors appeared to matter most of all: (1) thorough pre-experience preparation and post-experience follow-up; (2) the willingness of project staff to work overtime in finding suitable placements (achieved most easily if employers were friends of the teacher or of a pupil's family); (3) the maintenance of regular liaison between project staff and the employer; and (4) the support given by project staff to pupils who were struggling or failing in their placement.

Some of the innovative projects we visited were demonstrably evidence of successful practice in work experience. Examples were the work experience in a pottery which was set up within a unit (see p.36) and the vocational college for 14 – 19-year-olds (p.40). Staff in these situations were especially confident about their pupils' employability, maintaining that success in getting jobs or training places, even in areas of high unemployment, was as high or higher than among pupils in most local schools. The important element in the pottery factory project was that, to fulfil orders in time, pupils had to cooperate, even if this entailed undertaking boring tasks over several sessions.

Personal and Social Development

We examined three areas of pursuit related to pupils' personal and social development: 'club activities', PSE courses, and counselling. There was no doubt in the minds of most project staff that times set aside for pupils to play games, watch TV and listen to music were highly valuable. Some considered these 'club activities' successful in so far as they could be a useful carrot to keep pupils involved in more serious work; but much greater emphasis was placed on their facility for improving mutual understanding between staff and pupils and addressing pupils' personal problems. There was no consensus about the popularity of PSE courses, whether organized by project staff or outside agencies. When questioned about the importance of counselling as an aspect of project provision, there were different reactions depending on whether the counselling was formal or informal. Formal arrangements were believed to be very or quite important by about half the respondents, but a minority dissented from this view. In contrast, informal counselling, in terms of listening to pupils' concerns and building up positive relationships, was recognized as important by virtually everyone, most of whom expressed this belief strongly.

The bias in favour of opportunities for informal rather than formal counselling is not surprising. As professional counsellors often acknowledge, even adults with problems sometimes find it difficult to engage in the demands of formal counselling sessions. However, in deference to those with professional qualifications is counselling, we think that the term 'constructive listening' is perhaps a more accurate description of the kind of activity we are referring to. As pointed out in Chapter 6, comments made by project pupils as well as staff suggested that this is an aspect of the regime which was particularly valued. The fact that 'there was always someone to listen to you', as one group of ex-pupils put it, sums up the value everyone placed on this provision.

Links with FE

As we saw in Chapter 5, project leaders generally valued access to FE for their pupils, whom we were told could often realize success in a college setting even if they had a history of failure at school. Unfortunately, our evidence suggests that FE courses for Year 11 pupils are becoming harder to arrange as new charging arrangements by colleges now managing their own budgets make the cost prohibitive for some support projects. It is therefore all the more important to identify the conditions which seem to make prospects of success in FE more likely so that those course placements which are purchased will be value for money.

From our interviews, it appears that one of the factors influencing success in FE for project pupils was the nature of the target membership. Two aspects of this issue seemed to affect the ability of pupils to stay on course. One was that enrolling pupils for programmes which had been designed essentially for individuals with learning problems sometimes proved counter-productive. The level of work was often about right in theory. But, once they realized the nature of the target clientele, project pupils would sometimes say the course was too easy and remove themselves. Secondly, project pupils seemed more likely to stick with a course if no others from their group were on roll. In situations when other group members were present, any individual falling out could trigger off absenteeism among the others. At the same time, we found one successful example of FE courses which contained *only* pupils from local support projects. The key factor here was that the work programmes were specially designed for three off-site units within a six-mile radius of the college. With a total of around 80 pupils between them, the unit staff had been able to negotiate a choice of courses to meet effectively the need of the pupils.

2. Can Successful Off-site Practice be Transferred into Schools?

The demands of the National Curriculum are the main obstacles to schools adopting some of the strategies which have been used successfully in off-site units. Yet the possibility of incorporating successful off-site practice into mainstream provision is important to consider if schools are to reduce the number of pupils they exclude. It is easy to assume that few of the strategies used in small units are suitable for large mainstream schools. Our view, however, is that there are elements that can be considered for adaptation. In general terms, there is the question of styles of relationships – treating young people as adults, and avoiding the use of 'dominant' body language that is so often characteristic of teachers who are conscious of their role as persons in control of potentially unruly children. More specifically, we believe there is scope for schools to consider three sorts of activity which were addressed in our follow-up questionnaire and interviews: work experience, links with FE, and certain activities in off-site units. Indeed we chose to investigate these precisely because of their potential transferability into ordinary school settings. We turn now to discuss some of the issues and dilemmas which relate to the question of adopting these aspects of unit life as part of mainstream provision.

Work Experience

In principle, some of the strategies concerning business enterprises and work experience in off-site units would be workable in ordinary schools if there were sufficient interested staff. Unfortunately, the demands of an increasingly academic curriculum make it difficult to formalize arrangements for supervised and structured work experience. All the same, there are possibilities.

Work experience is already a feature of many Year 11 programmes in ordinary schools. However, although this activity is often highly effective, there is one particular feature of the arrangements found in off-site situations that is rare in mainstream provision. This is the flexibility of the timing of work experience, particularly the facility to arrange placements either as continuous blocks of time or on a part-time basis. In ordinary schools, the exigencies of the timetable and the subject-teaching responsibilities of work experience coordinators often make it necessary for placements to be limited to continuous blocks of time. This is usually satisfactory for pupils without special emotional or behavioural needs. But in the off-site situation, where by definition pupils have personal shortcomings, a degree of flexibility is high desirable. Many project workers explained the success of their placements in terms of the discretion they could exercise in planning blocks of experience for some pupils and one or two days a week for others. They also welcomed the opportunity to make alternative timing arrangements where earlier ones, whether block or part-time, proved too demanding for certain individuals.

Given the difficulties which schools face in accommodating flexible arrangements for placements to fit in with timetable constraints, it is worth asking if work experience on the school premises is a practicable proposition. One advantage of this arrangement is that the school would be more in control of the situation and better able to ensure special facilities and adaptable arrangements for pupils at risk of failing. In Chapter 4 we referred to two successful examples of on-site experience in project centres, one in which a pottery was set up and the other a garden workshop. We found that on-site experience could be particularly valuable when there were insufficient placements available to meet the demand, and also for pupils whose dress style turned out to be unacceptable to employers. Some schools already successfully organize on-site work by helping pupils to organize mini-enterprises. Perhaps an extension of this idea would meet the criteria of flexibility, which seems so important for pupils with problems in personal relationships.

Club-type Activities

Given the importance attached to 'club' activities in off-site centres, both in terms of their potential for releasing built-up tensions and informal counselling, it seems worth considering how this type of provision might be incorporated into the regimes of ordinary schools. In one experimental study of secondary school behaviour problems (Lawrence *et al.*, 1984), the staff of one London school decided to let the pupils run a mid-week lunch-time disco as an opportunity to ease tensions. This was scheduled at the time of the week when discipline seemed least secure, and the innovation apparently was a success. However, what we have in mind here is the provision of facilities for games such as table-tennis and snooker, watching videos, or listening to tapes. We think that in schools where there are behaviour problems with a considerable number of Year 11 pupils, there could be value in experimenting with a 'club' during one or two lunch-times each week. Apart from its intrinsic value in releasing tensions, it would give staff the opportunity to sit down and chat to pupils informally about their own problems and the difficulties their families may be experiencing.

There would certainly be problems in setting up and running club facilities. The obvious difficulty would be finding the necessary funds. Another would be providing a suitable room, one which did not have a classroom atmosphere. It would also be important to have a set of rules agreed, and preferably drawn up, by all concerned. In this respect, it might be necessary to look carefully at the policy on smoking, which is sometimes tolerated in off-site settings.

Perhaps the main problem, however, would be supervision. Hard-pressed subject-teaching staff wrestling with the latest missive on budget constraints or the National Curriculum could reasonably claim that any kind of 'club' provision during school hours would impose unreasonable demands on their time and energy. However, it might be possible to enlist the cooperation of behavioural support teachers, many of whom are former members of the staff of off-site units and who transferred to mainstream education after their posts were wound-up. A 'club' setting could provide a suitable informal context for behaviour support staff to cater for individual needs with a degree of flexibility.

Most support teachers are familiar with the situation where plans are made to discuss a pupil's concerns and the individual fails to turn up at the arranged time. If contact were possible during a club session, the time of the support teacher would not be lost through some pupils not keeping appointments since there would be others there with whom work could be done. Alternatively, the opportunity could be taken to observe how pupils who are disruptive in class relate to their peers in informal contexts.

One support teacher, however, could not be expected to take full responsibility for both supervising the club activities and also undertaking informal counselling work. There would therefore be the need for further help, and here it might well be possible to bring in other kinds of support staff, such as lunch-time supervisors, or individuals from outside the school such as those on pre-service training courses or from the welfare services. The experience would be excellent for young men and women training to be teachers or social workers, while education social workers who relate well to young people might also be willing to become involved in club sessions, just as they sometimes are in comparable off-site settings.

Although many teachers feel safer when there are very well-defined barriers between staff and pupils, outside the school setting many of the barriers between people with different roles are breaking down. Certainly this is the experience of Year 11 pupils who join FE courses, where the atmosphere is generally more open. Many younger teachers are willing to be more accessible to pupils during at least certain times in the week, but they need support to do this in a way which will not affect their professional status in a time of change. Perhaps the school club would help to establish appropriate communication styles between teachers and taught in a safe, controlled setting where there is no risk of one party taking advantage of the other.

If pupils who would otherwise be excluded from school are to be contained in mainstream education, it is difficult to see how integration can be expected to work without some concessions to strategies which have been effective in off-site settings. In Year 11, freer relationships between teachers and pupils can be fraught with misunderstandings, ambiguity and pitfalls; yet carefully and imaginatively managed, they can be extremely valuable.

'Constructive Listening'

As we have seen, our evidence clearly shows that informal counselling, or 'constructive listening' as it might be better called, is a particularly important aspect of off-site provision and could be a valuable by-product of 'club' sessions in mainstream settings. We turn now to examine in more detail the staffing implications of this kind of initiative.

In all education establishments there are always some teachers to whom youngsters are more inclined to turn in time of trouble. They are the people who are prepared to give time to listen. Sadly, the demands of the recent Education Acts make it increasingly difficult for school staff to set aside time for patient 'listening' to the concerns of individual pupils. Given that this facility can be a lifeline for pupils with personal problems, however, it behoves schools to ensure that such support continues to be available. At a time when teachers are being made redundant as a consequence of schools' financial difficulties, it might seem unrealistic to consider using valuable staff time for pupil counselling. However, there is a growing awareness of the increasing number of pupils in school who are vulnerable because of their family or community situation. Provision to relieve personal tensions is not only important for the sake of pupils' mental health but also for their academic attainment, since the reason why some pupils underachieve at school is no doubt because of their personal problems. Perhaps the availability of effective informal counsellors on school sites would obviate the necessity for more costly off-site provision.

One possibility might be for the 'natural counsellors' among the staff to be identified, and money for them to be set aside in the school budget for suitable INSET training. Given that 'constructive listening' generally takes place during break and lunch times and after school rather than through withdrawing pupils from class (which, if done routinely, would be inconsistent with integrationist principles), staff who specialize in this work should be given extra non-contact time in compensation. Inevitably, even in schools with 'club activities', pupils would need to make appointments during these times, but they should not have to wait more than a couple of days at most. They would know that they would then have undivided attention and a set amount of time to themselves.

Our view is that the staff who already show aptitude and willingness for this kind of work, rather than candidates from outside the school, should be the ones who are invited to become counsellors. While sometimes there is a case for bringing in well-qualified and experienced counsellors, the success of their work is inevitably restricted at first by the need to establish credibility among pupils, and this might take some months to achieve. Outside appointments also carry the risk of counselling being seen as one more way of aspiring to a job outside the classroom, whereas the most effective counsellors in schools seem generally to be those who are intimately aware of all aspects of the school's idiosyncratic life.

Links with FE Colleges

In spite of the current difficulties about the level of charges now being made for enrolment in FE courses, we found that prospects for pupils' success were generally regarded as high provided certain conditions, as outlined earlier, were met. On this argument, it would seem feasible and appropriate (budget considerations permitting) for ordinary schools to arrange links for Year 11 pupils with the local FE college, not least because success in that setting is often realized by individuals who have failed in curriculum work at school.

The special arrangement at one North London authority, which we described in Chapter 5, has much to commend it. Disaffected pupils during their last 15 weeks at school attend a tailor-made modular course, run jointly by support staff and college lecturers and located in college rooms set aside for the purpose. There seemed no doubt to us that the flexible opportunities afforded for both work experience and personal and social development were generally well-received by those attending.

Inviting Local People to Act as Mentors

Lastly, we commend an idea for mainstream schools which comes not from experience of off-site units but from the Cities in Schools initiative. This involves finding local people to act as mentors to those young people who lack strong significant adults in their lives. As evidence from work with disadvantaged adolescents has repeatedly demonstrated, it is relationships which are at the heart of the problem. The success of a system of mentoring in the USA is described by Butting and others (1992) in a recent book called *At-Risk Pupils in At-Risk Schools*. The account reveals how those concerned with troubled young people, but stretched to the limit with their school or college duties, were helped by volunteers from the community who worked with the family as well as with the pupil in trying to break a pattern of truancy.

58

3. Is There Still a Case for the Off-site Unit?

In Chapter 1, we drew attention to the argument that the growth of off-site units in the late 1970s and early 1980s was prompted most of all by the mainstream schools' urge to be rid of pupils with whom they could not cope and whose behaviour was having adverse repercussions on the learning opportunities of other pupils. Today, this situation is compounded by the need for schools to maximize their public image in order to attract pupils and an enhanced budget. As we go to press, it seems likely that the Education Act 1993 will oblige all LEAs to set up special institutions for excluded pupils. Is the case for such a statutory duty well-founded?

Although some of the submissions to the Elton inquiry argued for an increase in the number of off-site placements, the Committee rightly resisted going along with this view, not least because there was no evidence to suggest that discipline was any better in schools which have access to units. On the contrary, what data there was suggested that setting up units had made no impression on rates of exclusion even when variations in pupils' background and behaviour at entry are taken into account. It remains true, unfortunately, that many schools have yet to formulate effective whole-school policies which place less emphasis on reprimand and punishment and more on pre-empting behaviour problems and reinforcing wanted behaviour. But that is not a good argument for retaining off-site provision, only a reason for all schools to ensure that they introduce intervention strategies which are regularly reviewed for their effectiveness.

It has now generally come to be recognized that off-site provision cannot be justified for mainly negative reasons, especially when units are not in a position to deliver the National Curriculum. If they are to remain in any shape or form, they must be based not only on reasons relating to the good they can do for disaffected pupils, but on the grounds that some of the most effective approaches in off-site provision are not a practicable proposition in ordinary schools. In the previous section we suggested possible ways in which some key off-site strategies might be incorporated into the mainstream, so reducing the need for off-site units. The question we now ask is whether there still remains a case for these units or whether they should be regarded as redundant. Obviously, the answer depends on the quality and range of strategies which schools and local authorities are developing.

In one East London authority, we found that an initiative had been taken by an individual teacher who until recently was running an off-site unit. He was now putting his efforts into negotiating with the schools ways in which long-term non-attenders might be reintegrated. He described his work as like that of a salesman trying to sell a hard-to-shift product! It time, however, he had managed to persuade some schools to offer a flexible programme for persistent non-attenders, and he was now giving the pupils his full support by helping them to meet the curriculum, uniform and homework demands of the school. Some remarkable success had been achieved, with some of the pupils concerned obtaining good grades in maths and English GCSE in less than a year.

We need individuals such as this teacher to encourage innovation in schools, but clearly the initiative must not be left to chance 'salesmen'! Our view is that every education authority, or clusters of schools, should develop a continuum of flexible provision. A few innovative authorities have already done this. We found one example which seems to represent a model of its kind and which in principle could spell the end of the off-site unit. Unfortunately, as we shall explain later, the arrangements have recently fallen through.

In this scheme, each school has at least one 'liaison worker' who is both a member of the authority's support service team and a member of school staff. A liaison worker in a school works in a variety of ways, sometimes with individual pupils, sometimes groups, sometimes with whole classes, sometimes advising teachers. The flexibility of the scheme is demonstrated by the support given in one school where staff were experiencing many behavioural problems in nearly all their lessons with a particular group of children. To deal with this case, several liaison workers were withdrawn from their home school to tackle the problem as a team. For two weeks they worked intensively with the pupils concerned, identifying and addressing each area of concern. Apparently this 'task force' type operation was so successfully executed that other heads began to make requests for similar intervention to deal with behavioural problems involving whole classes.

The main aim of the liaison team members is to keep pupils in schools by providing all the help they can. Although the authority still runs a well-established off-site unit, it is envisaged that this provision can eventually be phased out. Already, its use is carefully controlled and restricted. At the time of our investigation, the mornings were used for the education of a few Year 11 pupils, and in the afternoons the unit acted as a temporary exclusion centre for a few pupils belonging to Years 7 to 10. However, the arrangement was that the pupils collected instructions for work from their school, and all the work accomplished in the unit had to be returned to the school for marking. This rule had two purposes: to ensure that the schools retained full responsibility for their off-site pupils and also that the pupils continued with the school's curriculum programme without serious interruption. At all times referral to the unit was seen as a temporary 'cooling off' measure.

At the extreme end of this authority's continuum of pupils with behaviour problems is a minority of individuals who have refused to attend the off-site unit. In these cases, individual ('home') tuition teachers meet pupils on their own territory, perhaps a wall at the end of an estate or on the town hall steps. The general aims of this 'I'll come to you' approach is to prepare the youngsters for return to education via a Friday afternoon session at the unit and to prepare them for work by arranging and supervising work experience and giving help in job applications. We described this latter aspect of the service in Chapter 4.

Similar initiatives to those described in this example have been developed in other parts of the country. Perhaps the main difference between those and this one was the degree of flexibility in returning the pupils to school and in changing the role of the liaison teachers for short periods as needs arose.

Unfortunately, the funding for this project is due to end in March 1993 and many of the team staff have left because of insecurity. At the same time, several of the feeder schools have become grant-maintained and seem more willing to exclude pupils, thus re-creating the need for an off-site unit. We have also learned of a number of other similar projects which are now threatened because increased delegation of funds to individual schools and opting-out is severely paring centrally-held LEA funds. The amounts left are little more than is needed to finance statutory statements of special educational need. The danger, as the Secondary Heads Association (1992) has warned, is that the changes in funding arrangements will lead to more excluded pupils being unable to find other schools that will accept them and so passing into a 'phantom zone'.

Notwithstanding this state of affairs, our conclusion is that there is still a place for the off-site unit provided it is used in a limited and flexible way and as part of a continuum of support provision, such as in the example just described. To this extent we are in agreement with the Elton Committee, who, after reviewing the pros and cons of alternative provision and support teams working in schools, concluded: ' We consider that the balance of advantage lies with the support teams' (DES, 1989, para. 6.49); but as Elton also acknowledged, so long as schools have the right to exclude pupils as a last resort and the LEA has the legal obligation to provide places for pupils permanently excluded, then it is probably necessary to retain some minimal off-site provision 'providing special help for those pupils who can, at least temporarily, be no longer constructively educated in ordinary schools' (para. 6.55). As in the example we gave, the role of the units should now be much more circumscribed, with access to them rendered less necessary by the development of pro-active policies in schools and through local authority support teams which are able to work in a flexible way. All this, however, assumes that adequate funding is available.

These conclusions assume that schools will be more willing to accommodate the kinds of practice which off-site workers have successful used. In our interviews, many staff from support projects expressed their doubts at ever being able to work so effectively within mainstream schools because of the lack of flexibility to use alternative methods to engage the motivation of reluctant learners. There remains the important question, therefore, of how encouragement can be given to schools to introduce more flexibility in their arrangements for dealing with disaffection.

One of the main objections to trying an innovative approach for pupils with behaviour problems in ordinary schools is that it would be resented by other pupils who are toeing the line despite having difficulties. However, if strategies can be offered for whole groups of pupils, this objection would be no longer valid. For instance, one source of disciplinary problem arises in making children from chaotic homes conform to the rules about school uniform. Although every school, in these times, has to sell itself, and although school dress is an important consideration in attracting recruitment, a school's public image need not suffer (and might even be enhanced) if older pupils could be involved in agreeing on a more relaxed, alternative form of dress. This is already the practice in some schools, and is general practice in most other Western countries.

Homework is another source of contention which can lead to disciplinary problems. Here again, pupils from over-crowded and disorganized homes are at a distinct disadvantage, as are those with no settled homes and those with short-term memories. Yet if homework is considered an important part of the school's policy, then there can be no exceptions. The school day is already long, but, given the argument that extra hours are necessary for successful achievement, some school or neighbourhood provision would help to solve this area of conflict. All pupils could have access to this provision, thus reducing the risk of stigmatization.

Flexibility is also needed to accommodate individual counselling and 'club' sessions; clearly schools would not want these facilities to be available as a 'sin bin' but to allow all pupils in Key Stage 4 to avail themselves of the facilities if they wanted to. Problems could then be identified and addressed earlier, thus obviating the need for 'crisis management' later on. There are naturally resource implications in implementing both these strategies, but, if the innovation proves successful, money spent on individual tuition might be saved.

As there are more and more reports of increasing numbers of pupils being excluded from schools because their unacceptable behaviour cannot be contained and is bad for the school image, lessons must be learned from those who have successfully engaged the interests of pupils in special provision. It is fashionable to place the blame for poor behaviour in school on the break-up of family life. But whatever merit there may be in this argument, perhaps we need to accept the fact that there are problems in society that schools could help to alleviate through a more flexible approach to education for a proportion of young people. The expression used most often by off-site workers when describing the success of their work was 'increase in self-esteem'; yet this is precisely what is at risk in schools which refuse to adapt their arrangements tomeet the behavioural needs of all their pupils. On present evidence, it seems unlikely that the escalation in exclusion rates can be stemmed without flexibility in schools' practices to enable our most troubled and troublesome pupils to find success.

In his conclusion to *How to Reach the Hard to Teach*, Paul Widlake (1983) wrote:

> The challenges from within and without are such that no school can continue to teach its present curriculum in an unchanged from. ...Being so heavily involved in certification, [schools] are bound to experience problems in devising programmes for pupils with special needs. The increasing disenchantment of some of these pupils provides an unanswerable case for fresh approaches. Such efforts should not be confused with 'softness' or sentimentality. (pp.122-3)

These words are true more than ever when, as we write a decade later, the curriculum of which Widlake speaks is being replaced by one of increased rigidity. The problems for disaffected pupils are further compounded by new statutory requirements to publish league tables, greater emphasis on pupil-led funding, and the creation of a two-tier system of council and centrally-maintained schools. In these circumstance, as we argued in Chapter 1, the increase in exclusion rates and pressure to increase off-site provision is not surprising. But if the spirit of the 1981 Act and the integrationist movement is to be maintained through attempts to reduce the number of children who receive education away from their peers, then both attitudes and the curriculum arrangements in mainstream schools will have to be examined. We also take the view that, since the exclusion problem is in part a product of national policies, a statutory duty for LEAs to set up special units is a woefully inadequate response to the problem. Some clear direction, backed by resources, is needed from the centre to encourage initiatives from LEAs and individual schools. The alternative is an increasing number of young people embarking on adult life with feelings of rejection and alienation from society.

APPENDIX A

Participating Authorities

Avon
Barking and Dagenham
Barnet
Barnsley
Bedford
Berkshire
Bexley
Birmingham
Bromley
Buckinghamshire
Calderdale
Cambridgeshire
Cleveland
Croydon
Devon
Durham
East Sussex
Enfield
Gateshead
Greenwich
Hackney
, Hampshire
Harrow
Havering
Hereford and Worcester
Hillingdon
Isle of Wight
Islington

Kent
Kingston upon Thames
Kirklees
Leeds
Leicestershire
Lincolnshire
Manchester
Merton
Newcastle upon Tyne
Newham
Northamptonshire
Northumberland
North Tyneside
North Yorkshire
Oxfordshire
Richmond upon Thames
Rochdale
Salford
Sefton
Sheffield
Shropshire
Solihull
Somerset
South Tyneside
Southwark
Stockport
Sunderland
Surrey

Sutton
Tameside
Trafford
Wakefield
Waltham Forest

Wandsworth
Warwickshire
Westminster
West Sussex

APPENDIX B

Institutions Visited

Bridge Educational Arts Centre, Warwickshire
Brighton Tutorial Centre, West Sussex
Cities in Schools, Piccadilly
Eastfield Centre, Sunderland
Edendale Centre, Gateshead
Islington LEA
Narborough Project, Leicestershire (now Leicester Support Service)
North Tyneside LEA
Oakfield Vocational College, Newcastle upon Tyne
Thorndale Centre, Cleveland
Three Mills Centre, Newham
Westlands School, Cleveland
Worthing Tutorial Centre, West Sussex

References

Advisory Centre for Education (1980) 'ACE Survey – Disruptive Units', *Where*, 158, 6-7.

Advisory Centre for Education (1992) 'Exclusions', *ACE Bulletin*, 45, 9-10

Audit Commission and HM Inspectorate of Schools (1992) *Getting in on the Act: Provision for Pupils with Special Educational Needs – the National Picture*, London: HMSO.

Basini, A. (1981) 'Urban schools and "disruptive" pupils', *Educational Review*, 33, 3, 37-49.

Bennathan, M. (1992) 'The care and education of troubled children', *Therapeutic Care and Education*, 10, 1, 22-34.

Butting, P.F., Corderio, P.A. and Prentice Baptiste, H. (1992) 'Philosophical and conceptual issues related to students at risk', in Waxman, H.C., Walker de Felix, J., Anderson, J.E. and Prentice Baptiste, H. (eds) *At-Risk Pupils in At-Risk Schools*, Berkeley CA: Sage Publications.

Cooper, P.W. (1992) 'Exploring pupils' perceptions of the effects of residential schooling on children with emotional and behavioural difficulties', *Therapeutic Care and Education*, 10, 1, 22-34.

Cooper, C., Upton, G. and Smith, C. (1991) 'Ethnic minority and gender distribution among staff and pupils with emotional and behavioural difficulties in England and Wales', *British Journal of Sociology of Education*, 12, 1, 77-94.

Daines, R. (1981) 'Withdrawal units and the psychology of problem behaviour', in Gillham, B. (ed.) *Problem Behaviour in the Secondary School*, London: Croom Helm.

Department for Education (1992a) *Choice and Diversity: A New Framework for Schools*, London: HMSO.

68

Department for Education (1992b) *Exclusions: A Discussion Document*, London: HMSO.

Department of Education and Science (1978) *Special Educational Needs* (Warnock Report), London: HMSO.

Department of Education and Science (1989) *Discipline in Schools* (Elton Report), London: HMSO.

Department of Education and Science (1990) *A Guide for Employers: Education at Work*, London: HMSO.

Docking, J.W. (1987) *Control and Discipline in Schools: Perspectives and Approaches*, 2nd edn, London: Paul Chapman.

Drew, D. (1990) 'From tutorial unit to schools' support service', *Support for Learning*, 5,1, 13-21.

Galloway, D., Ball, T., Bloomfield, D. and Seyd, R. (1982) *Schools and Disruptive Pupils*, London: Longman.

Galloway, D., Martin, R. and Wilcox, B. (1985) 'Persistent absence from school and exclusion from school: the predictive power of school and community variables', *British Educational Research Journal*, 11,1, 51-61.

Her Majesty's Inspectorate of Schools (1978) *Behavioural Units: A Survey of Special Units for Pupils with Behavioural Problems*, London; DES.

Inner London Education Authority (1985) *Off-site Support Centres*, Committe Paper 5042, London: ILEA.

Lawrence J., Steed, D. and Young, P. (1984) *Disruptive Children – Disruptive Schools?* London: Croom Helm.

Ling, R. and Davies, G. (1984) *A Survey of Off-Site Units in England and Wales*, Birmingham: City of Birmingham Polytechnic.

Ling R., Davies, G., Brannigan, C., Cooper, M., and Weston, B. (1985) 'A survey of off-site units in England and Wales', *CORE*, 9, Fiche 4/5.

Lloyd-Smith, M. (ed.) (1984) *Disrupted Schooling – The Growth of the Special Unit*, London: John Murray.

Lovey, J. (1991) 'The dilemma of entering disruptive and disaffected adolescents for external examinations', *Maladjustment and Therapeutic Education*, 9, 2, 75-82.

Lovey, J. (1992) *Teaching Troubled and Troublesome Adolescents*, London: David Fulton.

Lowe, P. (1988) *Responding to Adolescent Needs*, London: Cassell.

McDermott, J. (1984) 'A disruptive pupil unit: referral and integration', in Lloyd-Smith, M. (ed.) *Disrupted Schooling – The Growth of the Special Unit*, London: John Murray.

McManus, M. (1987) 'Suspension and exclusion from high schools: the association with catchment and school variables', *School Organisation*, 7, 261-71.

Mortimore, P., Davies, J., Varlaam, A. and West, A. (1983) *Behaviour Problems in Schools*, London: Croom Helm.

National Union of Teachers (1992) *NUT Survey on Pupil Exclusions*, London: NUT.

Nottingham Education Department (1991) *Pupil Exclusion from Nottingham Secondary Schools*, Nottingham County Council.

Office for Standards in Education (1993) *Education for Disaffected Pupils*, London: Ofsted.

Pyke, N. (1992) 'In to the exclusions zone', *Times Educational Supplement*, 26 June.

Secondary Heads Association (1992) *Excluded from School: A Survey of Suspensions from Secondary Schools in 1991-92*, Leicester: SHA.

Stiles, C. (1993) 'When the law plays its part in a pupil's future', *Guardian Education*, 19 January.

Topping, K. (1983) *Educational Systems for Disruptive Adolescents*, London: Croom Helm.

Whitty, G. (1984) 'Special units in a changing climate: agencies of change or control?', in Lloyd-Smith, M. (ed.) *Disrupted Schooling – The Growth of the Special Unit*, London: John Murray.

Widlake, P. (1983) *How to Reach the Hard to Teach*, Buckingham: Open University Press.

Index